DATE DUE

MAR ~~AUG~~ G VT

PATTERNS
and
MECHANICS
of
ECONOMIC GROWTH

A General Theoretical Approach

DAVID *Edward* CARNEY

 THE ANTIOCH PRESS

To

Helen,   Billy,   and   Vicki

and

Planners Everywhere

PREFACE

This book is an outgrowth of my thoughts on the process of economic growth and the problems confronting the macro-planner in developing countries. It is also a sequel to an article which I published in *The Indian Journal of Economics* (Vol. XLV, Part IV, No. 179, April 1965) under the title, "Incorporation of Replacement Capital in the Harrod-Domar Growth Model," in which my main interest was to derive an investment formula which incorporated depreciation, obsolescence, and technological as well as net investment, and could be used for planning purposes by macro-planners within the framework of the Harrod-Domar growth model. The attempt was partially successful in that such a formula was found, but it failed, unwittingly, to recognize that the formula could not harmonize with the notion of steady growth incarnated in the Harrod-Domar model. The discovery of its incompatibility with steady growth was the result of my attempt, subsequently, to elaborate a formula for growth which took as its starting point the assumption, obvious enough, that output, consumption, and investment do not, in general, grow at the same rate, and to fit my investment formula into this wider framework.

The main purpose of the book is an investigation of different patterns of growth of aggregate real output, consumption, and investment. The investigation reveals that all economies conform to one or the other of two main patterns of growth: $r_i > r_y > r_c$, or $r_c > r_y > r_i$, where r_y, r_c and r_i are respectively the rates of growth of aggregate real output, consumption, and investment. This conclusion is verified by data from a fairly representative sample of countries for which comparable data may be found in the United Nations *Yearbook of National Accounts Statistics*. All regions of the world are represented with the notable exception of the Soviet Union, China, and Eastern European countries, for which data are compiled on a different system and with different concepts from those employed by the United Nations. However, it can be verified that every country, including even socialist countries modeled on the Soviet pattern, conforms to one or other of the two main types of growth.

Part One of the book examines the principal characteristics of each type of growth with statistical verifi-
cation, the coefficients of growth, and the investment
and consumption programmes appropriate to each type,
within a framework of comparative statics—that is, on
the assumption of given values of r_y, r_c, and r_i.

Part Two is concerned with the dynamics of growth,
that is, with changing values of r_y, r_c and r_i, and examines the long and short term changes in the principal
coefficients of growth, the conditions for growth with
and without fluctuations, and the implications for a policy
of controlling the conventional business cycle. But business cycle theory, as such, is not discussed.

In Part Three some applications of the theory developed in the two preceding parts are discussed with
particular reference to the analysis of past patterns of
growth and to target setting in overall development planning.

Although qualifying Keynesian analysis at several
important points, the theory which the book elaborates
is firmly based on Keynesian income analysis in that
it does no more than give a comparative statistical
treatment of and dynamize the fundamental Keynesian
identity, $Y \equiv C + I$. My investigation was launched the
moment I recognized that the rate of growth of aggregate
output could be derived as a simple weighted average of
the rates of growth of consumption and investment and
that, consequently, these rates could each be expressed,
in turn, in terms of the growth rate of aggregate output.

As one familiar with but unaccomplished in the more
recent developments in mathematics, I have preferred to
use the simple tool of the compound interest formula
which can be found in arithmetic books, as well as the
elementary notions of the calculus, and to stretch their
use to the extent possible for my task. Fortunately, I
did not need much more in order to accomplish my
objective. The product is therefore recommended as
simple reading for the professional economist as well
as the general reader with the most elementary knowledge of mathematics—chiefly arithmetic and some elementary notions of the calculus.

For errors of interpretation or argument I must take full personal responsibility. I must also disclaim any connection or responsibility of the United Nations or its African Institute for Economic Development and Planning in regard to this work or the views contained therein. However, I gratefully acknowledge the benefits of discussion of several points with my colleague, Dr. Gamal Eleish of the Institute, while exempting him also from all responsibility for any views or errors.

Finally, I must record the satisfaction of my wife and children in seeing the book completed and in shape — a sort of compensation, to a small extent, for the enforced self-ostracism of many evenings and weekends for several months which the preparation of the manuscript entailed. It is the privilege of my readers and critics to judge the quality of the results.

D.C.

Dakar, Senegal
November, 1965

CONTENTS

PART TWO. COMPARATIVE DYNAMICS OF GROWTH

PART THREE. APPLICATIONS OF THE THEORY

PART ONE

COMPARATIVE STATICS OF GROWTH

PATTERNS OF GROWTH

The growth formulae of Professors Harrod[1] and Domar[2] initiated the contemporary interest of the economics profession in the conditions of steady growth and the causes of deviations therefrom. Thence interest has progressed to the formulation of cyclical models of economic growth in an attempt to understand the complex causes of the business cycle and to work out measures for its control. Our objective in this work is a more modest one than the construction of cyclical models but, at the same time, of general interest in that it aims at the formulation of a general theory of the patterns and mechanics of economic growth.

Our starting point is the income formula of Keynes presented in comparative static terms. We assume a closed economy or, more generally, an open economy in which the net effects of foreign trade are subsumed in gross investment. This is the simplest way in which foreign trade could be handled in the theory. A more sophisticated approach, if the data are available, would be to classify net foreign trade partly under aggregate consumption and partly under aggregate investment in those cases where this classification is relevant—chiefly those cases where there is an excess of imports over exports. However, the simpler approach is adopted in this paper, and net foreign trade is added to domestic investment to give the total of aggregate investment.[3]

---

1. R. F. Harrod, "An Essay in Dynamic Theory," *The Economic Journal*, XLIX (1939) 14–33.
2. Evsey D. Domar, "Expansion and Employment," *The American Economic Review*, XXXVII (1947) 34–55.
3. Effectively, this means that in order to make the theory applicable to both closed and open economies we cannot, properly, work with the conventional concept of GDP but with the concept of Gross Available Product (GAP) which differs from the GDP in that the *absolute* rather than the algebraic difference between exports and imports is included in computing the gross product of an economy. However, most of the available data on the growth of real gross product of various countries relate to the GDP and, except for a few obvious cases, the use of such data does not make much difference to the theory which is developed or to the results of its application.

This procedure (or its alternative) is designed to make the theory generally applicable to different economic systems.

The fundamental income formula is

$$(1+r_y)^t Y_0 = (1+r_c)^t C_0 + (1+r_i)^t I_0 \qquad (1)$$

where Y_0, C_0, I_0 are the aggregate real income, consumption, and investment at constant prices in base year zero, and r_y, r_c and r_i are the respective rates of growth of these magnitudes over a given period, t. Consumption and investment are assumed to grow at different rates on which the growth of income depends as a resultant. The value of r_y can be derived in year one as a simple weighted average of the rates of growth of consumption and investment with respect to the base year:

$$\text{In year 1,} \qquad (1+r_y)Y_0 = (1+r_c)C_0 + (1+r_i)I_0 \qquad (i)$$

$$\text{and in year 0,} \qquad Y_0 = \qquad C_0 + \qquad I_0 \qquad (ii)$$

Subtracting the second from the first equation we obtain

$$r_y = \frac{r_c C_0 + r_i I_0}{Y_0} \qquad (2)$$

The rate of growth of Y, r_y, is assumed to consist of the two elements, r_p (the rate of growth of population) and r_w (the rate by which the growth of income exceeds the growth of population, whether this excess is natural or planned).

$$\text{Hence,} \qquad r_y = r_p + r_w \qquad (3)$$

As in the analysis of Keynes, the growth of consumption is as important for the growth of aggregate income as the growth of investment, and interest centres on both as manipulable factors. Planners, however, are usually more interested, as was Keynes, in investment as the crucial factor in income growth. But this is a mistake which is, more often than not, a handicap to the planning process and to growth. Consumption can only be neglected at the peril of the plan, for consumption, like investment, needs to be planned if investment is not to be jeopardized — and vice versa.[4]

From equation (2) it is obvious that:

$$r_i = \frac{r_y Y_0 - r_c C_0}{I_0} = r_y + \frac{C_0}{I_0}(r_y - r_c) \tag{4}$$

$$\text{or, } r_c = \frac{r_y Y_0 - r_i I_0}{C_0} = r_y + \frac{I_0}{C_0}(r_y - r_i) \tag{5}$$

When we attempt to plot the growth curves given by either of the two preceding equations we find several solutions which correspond to various types or patterns of growth, as follows:

Type I: $r_c < 0$; $r_i > r_y \dfrac{Y_0}{I_0}$, i.e. $r_i > r_y \left(1 + \dfrac{C_0}{I_0}\right) > 2r_y$

(since, normally, $C_0 > I_0$)

---

4. J. K. Galbraith, not so long ago, stressed the importance of the planning of consumption, particularly in regard to its composition. He believes that collective consumption is too often neglected. While this point is not examined in this paper, it is an important one for the success of the planning of aggregate consumption. For the ability to hold down consumption to a planned volume may well depend for its success on its composition. Collective consumption has the merit that individual consumers have no control over its volume, so that it can more easily be adhered to as planned. (See Galbraith, *Economic Development in Perspective*, Harvard University Press, 1962, 43–45.)

hence, generally, $\quad r_i > r_y \dfrac{Y_0}{I_0} > 2r_y > r_y > 0 > r_c$

Type II: $\quad r_c = 0; \quad r_i = r_y \dfrac{Y_0}{I_0} = r_y \left(1 + \dfrac{C_0}{I_0}\right) > 2r_y$

(since, normally, $C_0 > I_0$)

hence, generally, $\quad r_i = r_y \dfrac{Y_0}{I_0} > 2r_y > r_y > 0 = r_c$

Type III: $\quad r_y > r_c > 0; \quad r_y \dfrac{Y_0}{I_0} > r_i > r_y$

hence, generally, $\quad r_y \dfrac{Y_0}{I_0} > r_i > r_y > r_c > 0$

Type IV: $\quad r_c = r_y = r_i$

Type V: $\quad r_y \dfrac{Y_0}{C_0} > r_c > r_y; \quad r_y > r_i > 0$

hence, generally, $\quad r_y \dfrac{Y_0}{C_0} > r_c > r_y > r_i > 0$

Type VI: $\quad r_c = r_y \dfrac{Y_0}{C_0}; \quad r_i = 0$

hence, generally, $\quad r_c = r_y \dfrac{Y_0}{C_0} > r_y > 0 = r_i$

Type VII: $\quad r_c > r_y \dfrac{Y_0}{C_0}; \quad r_i < 0$

hence, generally, $\quad r_c > r_y \dfrac{Y_0}{C_0} > r_y > 0 > r_i$

It can be determined, at a glance, that Types I-III belong to the same pattern where $r_i > r_y > r_c$, and Types V-VII to the same but different kind of pattern where $r_c > r_y > r_i$, with Type IV constituting the dividing line between these two main patterns.

Type I is ruled out as incompatible with growth. With a growing population and declining consumption while (theoretically) investment increases, there can be only one result—disaster. Such would be the case, for example, where $r_i = r_y \dfrac{Y_0}{I_0} + \theta$ and, consequently, $r_c = -\theta \dfrac{I_0}{C_0}$

Type II is also ruled out as incompatible with growth since, with a growing population, it involves a decline in per capita consumption and, therefore, in overall living standards. (This case is conceivable where a country concentrates on scientific progress and armaments at the expense of civilian consumption.)

Type III is compatible with growth of per capita consumption and overall living standards, but only if $r_c > r_p > 0$. Thus the general condition for this case can more accurately be written as

$$r_y \frac{Y_0}{I_0} > r_i > r_y > r_c > r_p > 0$$

The rates of growth of C_0 and I_0 can be specifically determined for this type, assuming that

$$r_i \doteq r_y + \alpha r_y (Y_0/I_0 - 1), \ r_i$$

lying in the range $r_y Y_0/I_0 - r_y$ and therefore $1 > \alpha > 0$.

Simplifying this value of r_i we find that

$$r_i = r_y (1 + \alpha \frac{C_0}{I_0})$$

and therefore,

$$r_c = r_y (1 - \alpha)$$

It can also be shown that $r_c > r_p$ provided $\alpha > r_w/r_y$.

A special example of this type is where $r_i = r_y \dfrac{Y_0}{C_0}$ and

$r_c = r_i (1 - \frac{I_0}{C_0})$. It can be easily demonstrated that for

these values of r_c and r_i, $r_y > r_c > r_p$, and $\alpha = (I_0/C_0)^2$.

Type IV is the steady-growth state propounded by Harrod and Domar. This, as will be seen subsequently, is a rather special case of growth, not the normal case.

Type V is the inverse of Type III and also compatible with growth. Specifically for this case, $r_y \frac{Y_0}{C_0} > r_c > r_y$; that is, $r_y(1 + \frac{I_0}{C_0}) > r_c > r_y$. The value of r_c must therefore lie in the range $r_y(1 + \frac{I_0}{C_0}) - r_y$. Therefore let $r_c = r_y$

$$+ \sigma \left\{ r_y (1 + \frac{I_0}{C_0}) - r_y \right\} , \text{ where } 1 > \alpha > 0. \text{ Then,}$$

$$r_c = r_y + \alpha r_y (\frac{Y_0}{C_0} - 1) = r_y + \alpha r_y \frac{I_0}{C_0} = r_y (1 + \alpha \frac{I_0}{C_0})$$

To obtain the value of r_i for this case we write

$$r_y Y_0 = r_y (1 + \alpha \frac{I_0}{C_0}) C_0 + r_i I_0$$

that is, $r_y \left\{ Y_0 - (1 + \alpha \frac{I_0}{C_0}) C_0 \right\} = r_i I_0.$

or, $r_y (I_0 - \alpha I_0) = r_i I_0$

then $r_i = r_y (1 - \alpha)$

Thus the values $r_i = r_y(1 - \alpha)$, $r_c = r_y(1 + \alpha \frac{I_0}{C_0})$, where $1 > \alpha > 0$ will always satisfy this case.

Types VI and VII are similar in that in both these cases aggregate consumption increases faster than aggregate income while aggregate investment increases less than aggregate income. This is also true of Type V,

but with the difference that in Type V the rate of growth
of investment exceeds zero while in Types VI and VII it is
respectively equal to, and less than, zero. Types VI and
VII are theoretically, as well as practically, possible
especially if foreign trade makes up for the deficiency in
investment by means of a rising net import of consumer
goods, presumably on the oasis of grants and other forms
of aid. But they could also occur through a more intensive
use of investment (e.g. through an increasing labour-
capital ratio as population grows, especially if $r_p > r_i$),
or through increasing disinvestment (domestic and foreign) for the purpose of maintaining consumption. These
devices, however, cannot continue to be used indefinitely
and, sooner or later, the growth of aggregate income must
come to a standstill and then decline. Type VII, like Type
I, is definitely incompatible with growth.

These two cases are therefore incompatible with
long-term growth implying, as they do, the possibility
of no growth and decline.

An example of Type VII is where $r_c = r_y Y_0/I_0$, and
$$r_i = r_y \frac{Y_0}{I_0} (1-C_0/I_0), \quad \text{so that} \quad r_i = r_c(1-C_0/I_0) \text{ and}$$
$$r_y Y_0/I_0 = r_c > 2r_y > r_y Y_0/C_0 > r_y > 0 > r_i = r_c(1-C_0/I_0)$$

Eliminating Types I, II, VI, and VII as either inimical
to growth per se, or incompatible with long-term growth,
we are left with Types III, IV, and V as the only cases
compatible with growth in the long run.

If long-term growth always follows the pattern of
Type III or Type V, the Harrod-Domar steady-growth
state (Type IV) would represent the floor of the growth
rate of investment and the ceiling of the growth rate of
consumption for Type III; alternatively, it would represent
the ceiling of the growth rate of investment and the floor
of the growth rate of consumption of Type V. In the same
way, we find that Type II growth is another limiting case
of Type III growth, representing the floor to the growth
rate of consumption and the ceiling to the growth rate of
investment for Type III growth. Likewise, Type VI
growth is another limiting case of Type V growth, representing the floor to the growth rate of investment and the

ceiling to the growth rate of consumption for Type V growth. Thus while we rule out Types I and VII as definitely inimical to growth and Types II and VI as incompatible with long-term growth, we do not need to consider Types I and VII except in connection with a different purpose, namely the theory of fluctuations, as distinct from the theory of steady and continuous growth. Nor do we need to consider Types II, IV, and VI any further in their own right, except as limiting cases of the two really important cases of growth, namely Types III and V. In the real world, however, long-term growth is unlikely to follow consistently or exclusively the growth pattern of Type III or Type V.

The conditions of steady growth are not normally possible except, perhaps, in a planned economy, while the growth conditions specified in Types III and V—that is, unequal rates of growth of output, consumption, and investment—are the normal conditions satisfied in the generality of cases. Furthermore, Types III and V are possible in both planned and unplanned economies, as evident in the different cases of France and Germany after World War II (see Table II). Moreover, even under a regime of planning, it is difficult to ensure that consumption and investment grow at the same relative rate for any considerable period of time. Especially in developing countries under the impact of the demonstration effect of higher consumption standards in the more developed countries, and the consequent pressure of the masses of their population for higher living standards (commonly referred to as "the revolution of rising expectations") it is manifestly difficult to maintain this equality of growth rates between the two main components of aggregate income, and even more difficult to prevent the rate of growth of consumption from rising above the rate of growth of aggregate income (Type V). Hence, the Harrod-Domar case may be regarded as a special case of growth, not the general case where unequal rates of growth of aggregate output and its components prevail.

The general conditions of growth, with the Harrod-Domar and other Types as limiting cases, may therefore be written as follows:

$$(1+r_y)^t Y_0 = (1+r_c)^t C_0 + (1+r_i)^t I_0 \qquad \text{(A)}$$

and *either*:

$$r_y Y_0/I_0 > r_i > r_y > r_c > r_p > 0 \qquad \text{(B) (Type III)}$$

subject to:

$$\text{(i)} \quad r_i = r_y Y_0/I_0; \; r_c = 0 \qquad \text{(Type II)}$$

and

$$\text{(ii)} \quad r_i = r_y = r_c \qquad \text{(Type IV)}$$

as limiting cases

or,

$$r_y Y_0/C_0 > r_c > r_y > r_i > r_p > 0 \qquad \text{(C) (Type V)}$$

subject to:

$$\text{(i)} \quad r_c = r_y Y_0/C_0; \; r_i = 0 \qquad \text{(Type VI)}$$

and

$$\text{(ii)} \quad r_c = r_y = r_i \qquad \text{(Type IV)}$$

as limiting cases.

II

GROWTH RATE CURVES AND COMPARATIVE EVIDENCE OF GROWTH PATTERNS

Growth Rate Curves

In order to plot the rates of growth of Y, C, and I for the Type III and Type V growth patterns, we must, first of all, assign arbitrary values to these quantities. All we really need is the ratio I/C (or its inverse) in base year 0. It does not really matter what value we assign this ratio as the curves will in all cases be of the same general shapes. Let us therefore assign the value $1/3$ to the ratio I_0/C_0.

Type III Growth

For this case,

$$r_i = r_y(1+ \alpha C_0/I_0), \quad r_c = r_y(1-\alpha), \text{ where } 1 \gtrless \alpha \geq 0$$

We may plot r_i and r_c in terms of r_y by assigning different values to α. Alternatively, we may plot r_y in terms of r_i, then in terms of r_c, varying the value of α. It is necessary to plot all these curves together in order to study their interrelationships. We shall assume that α increases and decreases progressively within the range $0 \leftrightarrow 1$ over successive time periods. This assumption is only made in order to facilitate the plotting of the curves and does not necessarily imply that in fact α so behaves. Otherwise the curves that we shall obtain are essentially timeless curves. Diagram I presents the shapes of the growth rate curves for Type III growth, including the limiting values $r_i = r_y = r_c$ (Type IV growth) and $r_i = r_y (1+C_0/I_0)$, $r_c = 0$ (Type II growth).

Type V Growth

For this case,

$$r_i = r_y(1-\alpha), \quad r_c = r_y(1+ \alpha I_0/C_0), \text{ where } 1 \gtrless \alpha \geq 0$$

Function	Time (Period)→ 0	1	2	3	4	5	6	7	8	9	10
	α →0	.2	.4	.6	.8	1	.8	.6	.4	.2	0
$r_i = r_y(1 + 3\alpha)$	$r_i = r_y$ X→ 1	1.60	2.20	2.80	3.40	4.0	3.40	2.80	2.20	1.60	1
$r_c = r_y(1 - \alpha)$	$r_c = r_y$ X→ 1	.80	.60	.40	.20	0	.20	.40	.60	.80	1
$r_y = r_i/(1 + 3\alpha)$	$r_y = r_i$ X→ 1	.62	.45	.36	.29	.25	.29	.36	.45	.62	1
$r_y = r_c/(1 - \alpha)$	$r_y = r_c$ X→ 1	1.25	1.67	2.50	5.0	∞	5.0	2.50	1.67	1.25	1

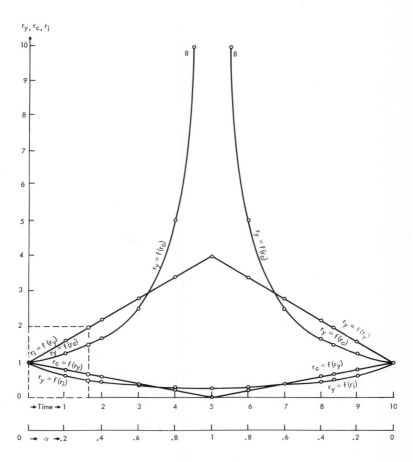

Diagram I. Type III Growth Rate Curves

Function	Time (Period)→	0	1	2	3	4	5	6	7	8	9	10
	α →	0	.2	.4	.6	.8	1	.8	.6	.4	.2	0
$r_i = r_y(1-\alpha)$	$r_i = r_y X$ →	1	.8	.6	.4	.2	0	.2	.4	.6	.8	1
$r_c = r_y(1+\alpha/3)$	$r_c = r_y X$ →	1	1.07	1.13	1.20	1.27	1.33	1.27	1.20	1.13	1.07	1
$r_y = r_i/(1-\alpha)$	$r_y = r_i X$ →	1	1.25	1.67	2.50	5.0	∞	5.0	2.50	1.67	1.25	1
$r_y = r_c/(+\alpha/3)$	$r_y = r_c X$ →	1	.93	.88	.83	.79	.75	.79	.83	.88	.93	1

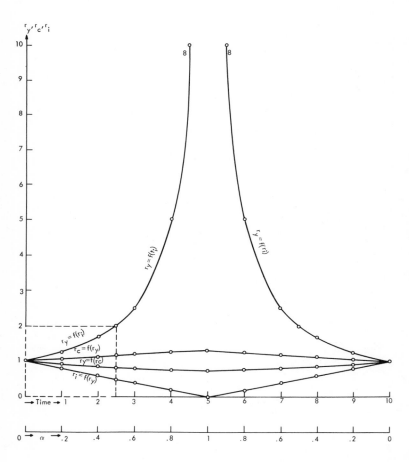

Diagram II.   Type V Growth Rate Curves

We follow the same general procedure as for Type III curves. But here the situation is the inverse or opposite of Type III growth and therefore the required curves will be those of Type III inverted. (Diagram II). In general, however, the ensemble of curves in both types of growth will have the same general appearance with the limiting values also inverted, except that the ceiling for the growth rate of consumption is lower in Type V than the ceiling for the growth rate of investment in Type III.

Statistical Evidence of Growth Patterns

All countries in the process of positive growth may be expected to conform to the main patterns of growth in Types III and V and to the underlying conditions. However, the conditions themselves do not enable us to distinguish between a "developed" and a "developing" country. Either type of country could exhibit the same pattern of growth, the difference between the two consisting in the degree of integration of interindustrial relations between the various sectors of their economies, and in the rate of technological progress. Thus a "developed" and a "developing" country could fall under the same pattern exhibited by Type III or Type V.

There is a fairly wide range of data which provide support for the approach to the theory of growth which has been adopted here, as well as a test of its usefulness in organizing countries according to the patterns of growth which they reveal. Such data have been assembled in Tables I and II, respectively for the countries commonly referred to as "industrial countries" and for those conventionally labelled "developing countries".

The first group of countries shows Types III and V patterns, the second group Types III, V, and VII; Type VII, as we have seen, being a limiting case of Type V. Thus the data are very much in accord with the expectations of the theory. Even the case of Puerto Rico, which is an apparent case of Type VII (although r_c for 1951-1959 should have been in excess of 6.6 and for 1953-61 in excess of 7.6) turns out to be a Type III when the computations are made on the basis of gross available, rather than gross domestic, product. The limiting case, Type VII, we have seen to be incompatible with long-run growth, and all the countries in the second group exhibiting this type of growth would certainly have a difficult future ahead of them if they were to continue in this pattern—with the exception of Puerto Rico because of its unique relationship with the United States of America, from which most of its investment is derived on account of the favourable inducements offered, including exemption from corporation tax for an initial period of ten years and from customs duties.

Growth is always possible, as the evidence shows, with or without a home-grown technology, so long as in the latter case technology could be borrowed or imported. Hence, developed as well as developing countries may exhibit the same pattern of growth as seen in Tables I and II. However, it seems clear that growth cannot become self-sustaining unless, and until, a country has established a scientific and technological tradition and regularly invests in the improvement of its technology.

The data in Tables I and II provide confirmation of what is already obvious: a given pattern of growth may be achieved with and without a régime of planning for the entire economy; for countries with varying economic policies and degrees of planning and non-planning are found among the two groups of countries. However, a knowledge of the conditions of the various patterns of growth should enable a country so inclined to undertake planning with more assurance than hitherto.

Developed versus Developing Countries

We are still without any criteria for distinguishing between developed and developing countries. We cannot derive any such criteria merely on the basis of growth rates and growth patterns. Indeed, other than the criterion of an established tradition of scientific research, technology, and technological progress, it is doubtful whether any other meaningful criteria can be established, and it is not proposed in this investigation to offer any. We may, however, re-examine the conventional practice

widely adopted in distinguishing between developed and
developing countries on the basis of per capita income
measured in terms of money at a given date.

A country may be said to be underdeveloped if its
per capita real income is lower than it need be, given
its actual and potential resources and the state of modern
technology. This definition may be accepted, implying
that a country's major bottleneck to development is the
backward state of its technology. There may, of course,
be other bottlenecks such as non-integration of its
economic sectors, inhibiting social attitudes, and other
institutional barriers to growth. However, the non-
integration (or imperfect integration) of its economic
sectors can be taken care of by an appropriate pattern of
investment, while the establishment of a tradition of technological progress and innovation may force social attitudes and institutional barriers into some accommodation
with this tradition. For, sooner or later, the acceptance
of a tradition of technological progress must imply, and
bring about with it, a more fluid social milieu and social
attitudes free from the trammels of confining customs,
traditions, and authority based on age groups and caste.

Growth itself may be defined as a process involving
a sustained and continuing increase in average, or per
capita, real income. And this implies that $\Delta Y/\Delta P$ is
always a positive quantity (where Y and P represent
aggregate real income and population, respectively) and
that population is not declining. For if population were
declining there could be a spurious growth of real per
capita income at an unchanged level of total output, or
at an increasing level of total output, although in these
cases $\Delta Y/\Delta P$ would not be positive, but zero and negative,
respectively. But the condition that population is not decreasing is still necessary in order to distinguish between the genuine and the spurious cases of growth.

These definitions of underdevelopment and growth
may therefore be regarded as fairly satisfactory.[1] When

---

1. Not quite satisfactory, however, if we are considering growth
of the components of the standard of living, that is, the level
of living. Then it is not enough for per capita income alone
to increase, but also per capita consumption and investment,
in real terms. (See Chapter III.)

TABLE I
INDUSTRIAL COUNTRIES' AVERAGE ANNUAL RATES OF GROWTH
OF REAL GDP AND ITS COMPONENTS (IN PER CENT)

| Country & Period | | GDP | | Expenditure on GDP | | | | | Implied Rate of Population Growth | Pattern of Growth |
| | | | | Consumption | | | Investment | | | |
		Total	Per Capita	Total[1]	Private	Government	Total[1]	Fixed Capital Formation		
I. E.E.C. Countries										
Belgium	1951–59	2.6	2.0	2.2	2.2	1.9	4.8	3.4	0.6	Type III
	1954–61	2.9	2.3	2.7	2.8	1.8	4.1	4.0	0.6	
France	1951–59	4.2	3.2	3.9	4.1	3.0	5.6	5.5	1.0	Type III
	1953–61	4.7	3.7	4.0	4.5	2.0	8.4	7.6	1.0	
Germany (West)	1951–59	7.3	6.1	6.8	7.4	4.9	8.6	10.1	1.2	Type III
	1953–61	7.0	5.7	6.7	7.0	5.8	7.8	9.9	1.3	
Italy	1951–59	5.7	5.2	4.6	4.3	6.8	10.3	8.4	0.5	Type III
	1953–61	6.0	5.4	4.7	4.5	5.7	12.6	9.2	0.6	
Luxembourg	1953–58	3.3	2.7	4.0	4.7	1.1	1.5	5.5	0.6	Type V
Netherlands	1951–59	4.6	3.4	3.8	3.9	3.2	7.3	6.5	1.2	Type III
	1953–61	4.8	3.4	4.2	4.6	2.6	6.6	7.1	1.4	

II. *Other*

										Type
Canada	1951–59	3.7	0.9	4.4	4.6	3.1	1.7	4.4	2.8	} Type V
	1953–61	3.6	1.0	3.7	4.3	1.2	3.1	2.9	2.6	
Denmark	1953–61	4.1	3.4	3.8	3.8	3.6	5.2	7.5	0.7	Type III
Japan	1954–59	8.3	7.2	6.4	6.5	6.1	13.6	17.9	1.1	} Type III
	1954–61	*9.9	*8.8	*7.0	*7.0	*7.3	*18.2	*19.9	1.1	
Norway	1951–59	3.3	2.3	3.0	2.7	4.4	4.2	3.8	1.0	} Type III
	1953–61	3.6	2.7	3.4	3.4	3.5	4.1	3.4	0.9	
Sweden	1951–59	3.4	2.8	3.2	2.9	4.6	4.0	5.7	0.6	} Type III
	1953–61	4.0	3.4	3.5	3.5	3.7	5.9	5.6	0.6	
United Kingdom	1951–59	2.6	2.1	2.4	2.7	0.9	4.0	5.7	0.5	} Type III
	1953–61	2.7	2.2	2.3	2.9	0.1	5.1	6.3	0.5	
United States	1951–59	2.8	1.1	3.2	3.3	3.2	0.8	2.1	1.7	} Type V
	1953–61	2.8	1.1	2.8	3.4	1.0	2.6	2.4	1.7	

Source: *UN Yearbook of National Accounts Statistics*, Part C & Part D, Table 2 A.

1 Figures in this column were computed by the author on the basis of the data given in the source. Changes in stocks are included.

* GNP at constant prices.

TABLE II
DEVELOPING COUNTRIES' AVERAGE ANNUAL RATES OF GROWTH OF REAL GDP AND ITS COMPONENTS (IN PER CENT)

Country & Period	GDP		Expenditure on GDP					Implied Rate of Population Growth	Pattern of Growth
			Consumption			Investment			
	Total	Per Capita	Total[1]	Private	Government	Total[1]	Fixed Capital Formation		
I. African Countries									
Algeria 1951–57	8.0	5.7	9.5	6.3	25.1	1.2	4.3	2.3	Type V
1953–57	10.0	7.7	12.3	7.4	33.0	-1.4	** 7.4	2.3	Type VII
Congo (ex Belgian)									
1951–58	4.9	2.5	5.8	5.7	6.1	3.3	3.0	2.4	} Type V
1953–58	3.8	1.5	4.3	4.2	5.1	2.7	-2.4	2.3	
Nigeria									
1951–56	4.1	-0.3	4.4	4.4	10.2	1.5	12.1	4.4	Type V
1953–56	3.0	0.9	3.8	3.4	13.1	-4.3	9.3	3.1	Type VII
§ 1953–56	6.1	3.0	4.1	3.7	13.6	21.8	10.6	3.1	Type III
Rhodesia & Nyasaland (Fed.)									
1955–59	6.8	4.1	4.9	4.7	6.9	12.5	2.0	2.7	} Type III
1955–61	5.8	2.9	4.6	4.4	6.1	9.5	-2.9	2.9	
II. Asian Countries									
Ceylon									
§ 1951–59	4.1	1.5	3.5	2.7	8.0	6.3	6.9	2.6	Type III
1951–59	3.0	0.4	3.7	3.2	7.6	-1.1	6.3	2.6	Type VII
1953–61	3.7	1.1	2.7	2.3	4.8	13.9	7.4	2.6	Type III
§ 1953–60	5.6	...	4.7	4.3	7.4	9.4	8.2	...	Type III
Israel									
§ 1956–59	7.1	2.4	6.8	9.0	-0.1	7.8	10.3	4.7	Type III
1956–59	*9.7	*5.0	*8.0	*8.8	*5.0	* 70.0	* 7.7	4.7	} Type II
1953–61	10.2	6.3	9.3	9.3	9.4	63.8	8.4	8.4	Type III
§ 1955–62	9.1	...	8.9	9.1	7.8	9.4	...	...	Type III
Korea (South)									
1954–59	5.1	2.8	4.0	4.8	6.3	6.6	7.0	2.3	} Type III
1954–61	5.4	2.0	4.2	4.2	4.6	10.4	4.9	2.4	

Philippines	§ 1952–59	5.6	2.3	5.4	5.1	8.5	7.7	11.5	3.3	Type III
	1951–59	*5.8	*2.5	*5.9	*5.6	*8.9	* 4.9	* 7.9	3.3	Type V
	1953–61	*2.6	*2.1	*4.8	*4.6	*6.6	*–26.5	*11.8	0.5	Type VII
	§ 1952–60	5.2	4.7	5.5	5.0	7.7	5.1	9.3	0.5	Type V
III. Latin America & Caribbean										
Chile	§ 1952–58	3.6	..	3.6	3.7	3.2	3.2	1.6	..	Type V
	1951–58	3.5	1.1	4.1	4.2	4.1	–2.3	2.4	2.4	Type VII
	1953–61	3.0	0.6	2.6	3.3	2.8	1.0	**6.5	2.4	Type III
Guatemala	1951–59	5.1	2.1	4.95	4.8	6.2	6.6	7.0	3.0	Type III
	1953–61	5.4	2.3	4.9	4.7	6.4	9.2	6.2	3.1	Type III
Honduras	§ 1951–57	4.3	1.1	4.8	4.7	5.6	2.3	4.2	3.2	Type V
	1951–57	3.6	0.4	5.2	4.9	9.4	–2.9	2.6	3.2	Type VII
	1953–61	3.7	0.7	4.0	3.8	6.6	2.1	–0.2	3.0	Type V
Jamaica	1954–58	8.9	6.9	7.8	7.6	9.0	16.2	10.0	2.0	} Type III
	1954–59	8.0	7.2	7.0	6.8	8.8	14.3	7.6	0.8	
Peru	§ 1952–58	3.5	0.9	4.7	3.9	10.9	–0.7	–0.1		Type VII
	1951–57	3.2	0.3	4.9	4.4	10.1	–2.2	0.7	2.3	} Type VII
	1953–57	2.7	2.3	5.2	4.5	10.6	–7.1	0.1	2.4	
	§ 1953–57	4.7		4.8	4.4	8.1	4.4	–0.3	2.4	Type V
Puerto Rico	§ 1951–57	4.7	4.1	4.7	4.1	8.3	4.9	8.1	0.6	Type III
	1951–59	6.1	5.5	ø4.9	4.7	6.7	–53.2	9.0	0.6	} Type VII
	1953–61	7.3	6.1	≠5.7	5.4	8.1	–19.1	9.7	1.2	
	§ 1954–60	4.6	3.4	5.1	5.0	6.2	3.5	8.1	1.2	Type V
Trinidad & Tobago	1952–58	9.1	5.9	8.7	9.6	3.6	10.5	13.8	3.2	} Type III
	1953–60	10.1	6.8	8.2	9.2	2.9	15.1	14.5	3.3	

Source: *UN Yearbook of National Accounts Statistics*, Part C & Part D, Table 2 A.

1 Figures in this column were computed by the author on the basis of the data given in the source. Changes in stocks are included.

* GNP at constant prices. ** Includes change in stocks. ø Should exceed 6.6. ≠ Should exceed 7.6.

§ Real GAP.

one examines, however, the conventional practice of
classifying developed and developing countries with
reference to an arbitrary figure of average money
income (the standard practice seems to employ a figure
of 300 U.S. dollars per capita as the dividing line) one
is compelled to object to this practice, convenient though
it may seem, on the ground that it implies a static
view of the growth process. Growth or development is a
dynamic process which becomes meaningful only when
discussed in terms of rates and patterns of growth of
aggregate real income, consumption, and investment,
rather than in terms of a static concept of per capita
income. This is especially true since a rising level
of real per capita income is the stated objective of
growth.

Our investigation of growth rates and patterns
therefore enables us to define growth and development
in this dynamic sense, while distinguishing the various
growth patterns which may result. On this view it
becomes more important to look at what is happening
to the growth rates of income, consumption, and investment within an economy, and between several economies,
over time than to rank them arbitrarily at a certain
point in time, with an implied but somewhat fallacious
view of some gap between countries that should be
bridged, no one seeming to know how.

Our analysis has revealed various patterns of growth,
the two most important of which, Types III and V, are
mirror images of each other with reference to the steady-
growth state. Professor W. Arthur Lewis has char-
acterized the central problem of economic growth in
the following terms:

> We have seen in the first section of this chapter
> that communities in which the national income
> per head is not increasing invest 4 or 5 per
> cent of their national incomes per annum or
> less, whilst progressive economies invest 12
> per cent per annum or more. The central
> problem in the theory of economic growth is
> to understand the process by which a com-
> munity is converted from being a 5 per cent
> to a 12 per cent saver - with all the changes

in attitudes, in institutions and in techniques which accompany this conversion.[2]

While questions may be raised concerning the validity of the percentages and the rather sweeping nature of the generalization, it may be conceded that the essential nature of the problem of growth has been aptly summarized by Professor Lewis, although he did not in his book proceed to an investigation of the mechanics of growth.

It is a part of our investigation here to examine the mechanics of the process of growth and it has become clear, up to this point, that not only the *rate* of saving (or investment) but also the *relative rates of growth of saving, investment, and consumption* are equally important in determining growth per se, as well as the pattern of growth which may result. This statement and its implications will become clearer as the investigation proceeds.

2. W. Arthur Lewis, *The Theory of Economic Growth,* Richard D. Irwin, Inc., 1955, Chapter 5, 225-6.

III
INVESTMENT PROGRAMME FOR THE DIFFERENT PATTERNS OF GROWTH

A. Deriving the Investment Programme

In a previous paper entitled "Incorporation of Replacement Capital in the Harrod-Domar Growth Model,"[1] I attempted to work out the general investment requirements for growth, making allowance for investment in replacement capital (defined as depreciation plus obsolescence), net investment for growth, and investment in technological progress or what the late Professor Sumner Slichter called "the science of discovery." Aggregate income, Y, was assumed to grow at an annual rate of G (= r_y, as defined in the first Chapter), k being the overall incremental capital-output ratio.

The current value of society's capital stock is then kY, a proportion of this, π, being replaced annually. This proportion π was found to have the value G^2, so that the volume of replacement capital R is given by the equation,

$$R = \pi \, kY = G^2 kY \qquad (6)$$

The volume of replacement capital was assumed to consist of two parts, one part on account of depreciation, the other on account of obsolescence. If μ represents the proportion of replacement capital due to depreciation, then the proportion due to obsolescence is found to be $1-\mu$. The further assumption was made that investment in technology bore some relationship to replacement capital and was, at least, equal in volume to that part of replacement capital due to obsolescence.

---

1. David Carney, "Incorporation of Replacement Capital in the Harrod–Domar Growth Model", *The Indian Journal of Economics*, XLV, Part IV, no. 179 (1965), 343–365.

Thus the coefficient of minimum[2] technological investment, τ, was found to be equal to $1-\mu$, so that the

---

2. *Idem.* It is more appropriate to call this the *marginal* technological investment. Total technological investment may be derived separately. Henceforth we refer to the coefficient of marginal (or minimum) technological investment simply as the coefficient of technological investment, or the technological coefficient.

It is possible, however, to demonstrate that, in fact, the required marginal technological investment is exactly equal to the required provision for obsolescence. Let marginal technological investment required in period 1 be M, which is needed to ensure the continued efficiency and technological advancement of the system of production. It must, like the provision required for obsolescence, bear some relationship to the amount of replacement capital, since obsolescence, the casualty of technological progress, is merely the reverse side of the coin of technological progress. Hence let it bear a ratio τ to the required volume of replacement capital R. If we represent depreciation by D, and obsolescence by O, we then have the following ratios:

$$\tau = \frac{M}{R}, \quad 1 - \tau = \frac{R-M}{R}, \quad \mu = \frac{D}{R} \text{ and } 1 - \mu = \frac{O}{R}$$

Because of the inseparable link between marginal technological investment and obsolescence, we may assume that the former bears to the latter the same relationship that depreciation bears to the quantity, $R-M$. Hence,

$$\frac{M}{O} = \frac{D}{R-M}, \quad \text{i.e.} \quad \frac{\tau R}{(1-\mu)R} = \frac{\mu R}{(1-\tau)R}$$

whence,

$$\tau - \tau^2 = \mu - \mu^2, \text{ or } \tau = 1-\mu$$

Alternatively, for the same reason of the close connection between marginal technological investment and obsolescence, we may assume that marginal technological investment bears to the quantity, $R - M$, the same relationship that obsolescence bears to depreciation. Hence,

$$\frac{M}{R-M} = \frac{O}{D}, \quad \text{i.e.} \quad \frac{\tau R}{(1-\tau)R} = \frac{(1-\mu)R}{\mu R}$$

whence, $\tau\mu = (1-\tau)(1-\mu)$, or $\tau = 1-\mu$, as before.

Hence, also, we see that $M = \tau R = (1-\mu) R = O$. That is, the required marginal investment for technological research and development must exactly equal the required allocation for obsolescence.

required marginal (i.e. minimum) volume of investment in technology was τR, where

$$\tau R = (1-\mu)G^2 kY \tag{7}$$

The volume of net investment (or increase in capacity) required to sustain an increase of G in aggregate income was assumed to be T, where

$$T = GkY \tag{8}$$

Thus the gross volume of investment, I, in a given year was found to be the sum of the three elements R, τR and T, so that

$$I = kG \left\{ 1+G(2-\mu) \right\} Y \tag{9}$$

Starting from base year 0, the investment programme for year 1 becomes

$$I_1 = kG \left\{ 1+G(2-\mu) \right\} Y_0 \tag{10}$$

Equation 10 was left in this form in the paper under reference,[3] for the sake of formal comparison with the Harrod-Domar formula so that, with the incorporation of replacement capital (and technological investment) in the formula, the required gross savings ratio $\acute{\sigma}$ becomes

$$\acute{\sigma} = I_1/Y_0 = kG \left\{ 1+G(2-\mu) \right\} \tag{11}$$

However, Equation 10 could be further simplified, since

$$kGY_0 = \frac{I_0}{\Delta Y_0} \cdot \frac{\Delta Y_0}{Y_0} \cdot Y_0 = I_0 \begin{array}{l}(=\text{net investment, T, in} \\ \text{year 1})\end{array}$$

and therefore could be written

$$I_1 = \left\{ 1+G(2-\mu) \right\} I_0 \tag{12}$$

a formula which is explicitly independent of the incremental capital-output ratio, k.

---

3. *Idem.*

It is clear from Equation 12 that the rate of growth of investment, r_i, is equal to $G(2-\mu)$. Therefore, generalized for any number of years, t, the investment formula becomes

$$I_t = \left\{ 1+G(2-\mu) \right\}^t I_0$$

or, replacing G by r_y,

$$I_t = \left\{ 1+r_y(2-\mu) \right\}^t I_0 \qquad (13)$$

Equation 13 applies equally to steady-growth as to any other type of growth. It is possible, however, to arrive at a slightly different, but equivalent, form of this equation in which r_y is replaced by π/r_y as follows:
As before,

$$R = \pi kY$$

τ, the coefficient of (marginal) technological investment is still equal to $1-\mu$, so that the required marginal volume of technological investment, τR, is given by

$$\tau R = (1-\mu) \pi kY$$

and the net investment T required to sustain an increase of r_y (or G) in aggregate income is given by

$$T = r_y kY$$

The gross volume of investment, I, for year 1, with respect to base year 0 is

$$I_1 = kY_0 \left\{ r_y+(2-\mu)\pi \right\} = kr_y Y_0 \left\{ 1+ (2-\mu)\pi/r_y \right\}$$

As before, $kr_y Y_0 = \dfrac{I_0}{\Delta Y_0} \cdot \dfrac{\Delta Y_0}{Y_0} \cdot Y_0 = I_0$, so that

$$I_1 = \left\{ 1+(2-\mu)\pi/r_y \right\} I_0$$

which, generalized for any number of years t becomes

$$I_t = \left\{ 1+(2-\mu)\pi/r_y \right\}^t I_0 \qquad (14)$$

which is the same as Equation 13. For, as we shall soon see, π is always equal to r_y^2 so that π/r_y is always equal to r_y, in every pattern or type of growth.

Having seen that there are only two main types of growth (III and V) with the other relevant types as limiting cases, we may now investigate the nature and requirements of the investment programme for the two main types giving special attention to the requirements of steady growth (Type IV) both on account of the general interest of economists in this particular type of growth and because of its rather peculiar implications for technological progress and technological investment. In our investigation of the three types of growth we shall use the generalized version of the investment programme given by Equation 14 in preference to that of Equation 13 in order to demonstrate that π is always equal to r_y^2.

Type III Growth: $r_y Y_0/I_0 > r_i > r_y > r_c > 0$

The investment programme in time t is given by

$$I_t = \left\{ 1+(2-\mu)\,\pi/r_y \right\}^t I_0$$

In this case,

$$r_i = r_y(1+\alpha C_0/I_0)$$
$$\text{and} \quad r_c = r_y(1-\alpha)$$

where $\alpha = (r_i-r_c)I_0/r_y Y_0$, and $1 > \alpha > 0$

It follows, therefore, that

$$(2-\mu)\,\pi/r_y = r_i = r_y(1+\alpha C_0/I_0)$$

that is, $(2-\mu)\,\pi/r_y = \left\{ 2-(1-\alpha C_0/I_0) \right\} r_y$

Since the expressions on both sides of the equation are of the same form and value, we may conclude that

$$\mu = 1-\alpha C_0/I_0$$

$$1-\mu = \alpha\, C_0/I_0 \qquad \text{(obsolescence coefficient or coefficient of technological investment)}$$

$$\pi = r_y{}^2$$

Or, again,

$$r_y(1+\alpha C_0/I_0) = \left\{1+ (1-\mu)\right\} \pi/r_y$$

with similar results as before for μ, $1-\mu$, and π.

All this implies that in a Type III economy with technological progress the depreciation coefficient is always less than unity and the obsolescence coefficent or coefficient of technological investment always has the value $\alpha\, C_0/I_0$. Furthermore, the growth rate of investment, r_i (which is the same as $(2-\mu)r_y$) represents the growth of investment necessary to cover replacement and technological investment, the net addition to society's capital stock being understood to be equal to the whole of the previous year's gross investment. In other words, given that the net addition to society's capital stock in any one year is always equal to the gross investment of the previous year, an additional increment of investment is only needed for the sole purpose of making provision for replacement and technological progress. Thus the growth rate of investment consists of two parts: r_y for replacement capital and $\alpha\, r_y C_0/I_0$ for the marginal technological investment.

Let us try to see what changes take place within a Type III economy as the value of α changes within the range $0 \leftrightarrow 1$. For this range of values for α it is clear that μ will assume values ranging from 1, when $\alpha = 0$, to below 0 or negative when $\alpha = 1$ (since normally C_0/I_0 is greater than unity, so that $\mu = 1-\alpha C_0/I_0$ must be negative). In general, $C_0/I_0 > 1$.

When $\alpha = 1$, $\mu = 1-C_0/I_0$, $r_i = (1+C_0/I_0)r_y$, $r_c = 0$

We then have a Type II economy in which r_i attains its maximum value (in excess of $2r_y$) and r_c its minimum value, zero. Here society is living on its capital but more than making up for it by a rapid obsolescence of capital, thereby fulfilling its replacement requirements.[4] But this type of economy, as we have seen, is ruled out as incompatible with growth. For with a growing population, but no growth in consumption, this can only mean disaster for such an economy.

$$\text{When} \quad \alpha = 0, \quad \mu = 1, \quad r_i = r_y = r_c$$

We then have the Harrod-Domar steady-growth state (Type IV economy) in which no technological progress is possible because there is no technological change, and no technological investment.

Avoiding these two extreme situations in which, respectively, consumption ceases to grow and there is no technological progress, a Type III economy must therefore have or select values of α such that $1 > \alpha > 0$, in order to retain its character and grow with a progressing technology.

There is, however, the crucial value, $\alpha = I_0/C_0$, when $\mu = 0$, $1-\mu = 1$, $r_i = 2r_y$ and $r_c = r_y(1-I_0/C_0)$. In this case society would be making no provision for depreciation, or capital consumption, but filling its replacement requirements entirely by the replacement of obsolete with up-to-date equipment. Above this value of α, the rate at which society runs down its capital stock increases (μ is negative, that is, depreciated capital is being brought back into service) and so does the retirement rate of obsolete capital (the obsolescence coefficient exceeding unity), which more than compensates for the deterioration of capital and enables the society thereby to meet its replacement bill. Below this value of α, the depreciation and obsolescence (or technological) coefficients are all positive and fractional. In general, the more α falls below the value I_0/C_0, the higher the (fractional) depreciation coefficient, and the closer its value approaches unity. At the same time, the obsolescence coefficient diminishes towards zero, and both r_i and r_c approach r_y, the one from above, the other

---

4. This may or may not be the case, much depending on the value of C_0/I_0.

from below the value r_y. This may be expressed in symbolic terms as follows:

$$\text{as } \alpha \longrightarrow 0, \quad \mu \longrightarrow 1, \; r_i \text{ and } r_c \longrightarrow r_y$$

that is, the steady-growth state is approached.

It may therefore be concluded that in Type III, since depreciation is normally a positive quantity, α can never equal or exceed the value I_0/C_0, so that r_i is always less than $2r_y$, and r_c always greater than $r_y(1-I_0/C_0)$. These conditions may be regarded as a set of consistency tests for the national accounts data of a country proceeding on a Type III growth pattern.[5]

The value $r_y(1-I_0/C_0)$ above which r_c must always lie also sets the maximum value for the rate of population growth (or the rate of growth of the labour force) in a Type III economy for real income and consumption per capita to increase continually, as well as investment per man, without jeopardizing capital replacement and technological progress. This point will be taken up later.

We may now write the investment programme in Type III as follows:

$$I_t = (1+r_i)^t I_0 = 1 + r_y (1 + \alpha C_0/I_0)^t I_0$$

The growth equation is then

$$(1+r_y)^t Y_0 = (1+r_c)^t C_0 + (1+r_i)^t I_0$$

i.e.,

$$(1+r_y)^t Y_0 = \left\{ 1+r_y(1-\alpha) \right\}^t C_0 + \left\{ 1+r_y(1+\alpha C_0/I_0) \right\}^t I_0$$

When $t = 1$, this becomes

$$(1+r_y)Y_0 = \left\{ 1+r_y(1-\alpha) \right\} C_0 + \left\{ 1+r_y(1+\alpha C_0/I_0) \right\} I_0$$

$$= \left\{ (1+r_y)C_0 - \alpha r_y C_0 \right\} + \left\{ (1+r_y)I_0 + \alpha r_y C_0 \right\}$$

---

5. By these tests some of the data for Type III growth in Tables I and III fare badly on the score of consistency.

or,
$$(1+r_y)Y_0 = (1+r_y)C_0 + (1+r_y)I_0$$

Thus the growth equation is in balance and shows clearly that the incremental contribution for technological investment must come from consumption in order that this balance may be achieved. The implication here seems to be that the incidence of technological progress in a Type III economy is largely in the investment-goods sector and that consumption must therefore subsidize the cost of technological progress in order that a higher rate of growth of investment (relative to aggregate income and aggregate consumption) may be achieved.

Type IV Growth: $r_i = r_y = r_c$

The investment programme in time t is given by
$$I_t = \left\{ 1+(2-\mu)\pi/r_y \right\}^t I_0$$
In this case,
$$r_i = r_y = r_c$$
It follows, therefore, that
$$(2-\mu)\pi/r_y = r_i = r_y$$
that is
$$(2-\mu)\pi/r_y = (2-1)r_y$$

Since the expressions on both sides of the equation are of the same form and value, we may conclude that
$$\mu = 1$$
$$1-\mu = 0$$
$$\pi = r_y{}^2$$

Thus the investment programme for steady growth becomes
$$I_t = (1+r_y)^t I_0$$
as should be expected.

Since the obsolescence coefficient, $1-\mu$, is 0 and is the same as the technological coefficient, we arrive at the rather startling conclusion that in the steady-growth state there is no obsolescence because there is no technological progress (the "state of the arts" being permanently unchanged) and therefore no need for technological investment. Technological investment, in short, is zero or, if made, would merely be wasted because it would not affect the existing state or level of technology so long as the condition of steady growth persists.

Steady growth, being therefore (at least in form) incompatible with technological progress, is clearly possible only in technologically backward and stagnant societies. Who then would want steady growth? Not even the backward societies of our contemporary world, for all of them wish to leap, if possible, into the twentieth century.[6]

---

6. This conclusion represents an important qualification to my earlier paper in which technological progress was assumed to be compatible with the conditions of steady growth, as in the Harrod-Domar theory. Consequently, the investment programme (including the marginal investment in technology on various assumptions for the value of $\mu < 1$) for each of the four countries examined in that paper was projected at the same rate of growth as total output. However, this procedure is now clearly seen to have been illegitimate, in theory and in fact; but only because of the more general approach to the theory of growth adopted here, in which we work with both r_y and r_i independently. Starting out with the general case and working out the investment requirements on the assumption that r_y and r_i are of different values, it becomes easier to see clearly the implications of steady growth by subsequently making r_i equal to r_y. Had this more general approach been adopted in the earlier paper instead of starting out on the assumption, implied in the Harrod-Domar case, that r_i and r_y are equal, it should have been easy to see at a glance that in the investment formula of equation 13, written in the form,

$$I_t = \left\{ 1 + G \ (2 - \mu) \right\} \ {}^t I_0$$

$G \ (2-\mu) = G$, and that automatically $\mu = 1$, leaving no place for obsolescence and technological investment.

If, however, from the outset the provision for marginal technological investment is included in consumption in Type III, and in investment in Type V, it is possible to obtain formalistic equations of steady growth in which $r_i = r_y = r_c$. One may then arrive at the opposite conclusion that steady growth is compatible with technological progress (as is assumed in the Harrod-Domar model) but required marginal and total technological investment would both become indeterminate since there would be no way of deriving marginal technological investment separately.

A further implication of the steady-growth state for Type III and Type V economies, where $r_i \neq r_y$, may be drawn from the fact that it is a limiting case of these two types. The implication is that the approach of these types to the steady-growth state may be regarded as an approach to a critical stage in the course of their growth, a point of inversion from which they should make all effort to pull back, or else pass quickly through to the opposite type. The steady-growth state thus represents the stage at which either type undergoes an inversion or transformation into the other, the stage at which, apparently, technological investment levels off at a plateau, technology remains the same, and technological progress is nothing more than a series of innovations, rather than a series of discoveries.[7]

Whether the transition of a Type III or Type V economy through the steady-growth state can be made with or without violent economic upheaval is an interesting question for speculation and further investigation. It seems very clear, however, more than before, that the steady-growth type is neither a normal nor a general type of growth, and is even less desirable, than is now generally thought, to be made an objective of growth or of general growth policy.

So far, we have been discussing only one type of steady-growth, the type where, in the general growth equation

$$(1+r_y)^t Y_0 = (1+r_c)^t C_0 + (1+r_i)^t I_0$$

$r_y = r_c = r_i > 0$. This is the Harrod-Domar type of steady growth. There is, however, another type of

---

7. It is possible, however, that for these types of economies the approach to the steady growth state may represent a period of intense scientific activity just before final break-throughs are achieved, permitting the resumption of the application of the new scientific results to the task of production. Thus, depending on how long is the gestation period of scientific research in progress, it seems possible for a Type III or Type V society to hover for a while around the steady-growth state before pulling back away from or passing through it into its inverse type.

"steady growth", where $r_y = r_c = r_i = 0$. It is steady growth only in the formal sense that $r_y = r_c = r_i$; but in fact it is not growth in a real sense because it is the classical case of equilibrium, the stationary state, where the rate of profit dwindles to zero and the same level of income, of consumption, and of investment is perpetuated eternally. Then we have the income equation of the stationary state

$$Y_0 = C_0 + I_0$$

which is the reference base of growth.

Type V Growth: $r_y \dfrac{Y_0}{C_0} > r_c > r_y > r_i > 0$

The value of the investment programme is given by

$$I_t = \left\{ 1 + \frac{(2-\mu)\pi}{r_y} \right\}^t I_0$$

In this case,

$$r_i = r_y (1 - \alpha)$$

and $r_c = r_y \left(1 + \alpha \dfrac{I_0}{C_0} \right)$ where $\alpha = (r_c - r_i) C_0 / r_y Y_0$, and

$$1 > \alpha > 0$$

It follows, therefore, that

$$(2-\mu)\,\pi/r_y = r_i = r_y (1 - \alpha)$$

that is, $(2-\mu)\,\pi/r_y = \left\{ 2 - (1+\alpha) \right\} r_y$

Since the expressions on both sides of the equation are of the same form and value, we may conclude that

$$\mu = 1 + \alpha$$
$$1 - \mu = -\alpha \text{(obsolescence coefficient or coefficient of technological investment)}$$
$$\pi = r_y^{\,2}$$

Or, again, $r_y(1-\alpha) = \left\{ 1 + (1-\mu) \right\} \; \pi/r_y$

with similar results as before for μ, $1-\mu$, and π.
   (i) $1 > \mu > 0$

In a technologically progressive society, however, the coefficient of obsolescence (or its counterpart, the coefficient of technological investment) is never a negative quantity. Hence if it is accepted that the depreciation coefficient is always less than unity, the negative sign of α, the obsolescence coefficient, then needs to be explained. It simply reflects the fact that in Type V growth provision for technological investment has to come out of funds allocated to investment; this is added to consumption, hence the higher growth rate of consumption relative to investment. The implication here seems to be that a Type V economy being consumption-oriented, the impact of obsolescence and technological progress is more in the consumption-goods industries than in the investment-goods industries. The rate of growth of consumption-goods industries and consumption-goods-oriented technological investment is therefore greater than that of investment-goods industries. By contrast, in Type III growth, which is oriented more towards investment-goods industries, the impact of obsolescence and technological progress is heaviest in the investment-goods industries. The provision for technological investment therefore comes from the allocation to consumption to increase the expenditures on investment goods and investment-goods-oriented technological research. Hence the higher rate of growth of investment relative to consumption.

In short, in a Type V economy the leading sector of growth is the consumption-goods sector, while in a Type III economy the leading sector is the investment-goods sector. In the one the investment-goods sector subsidizes the consumption-goods sector, in the other the consumption-goods sector subsidizes the investment-goods sector. This aspect of the growth rates of consumption and investment is explained further in Chapter IV where it is shown that the subsidy from one sector to the other in respect of technological investment and the corresponding adjustment for this in their respective growth rates leaves the balance of the general equation of growth unaltered.

Since in Type V growth the provision for technological investment is deducted from the investment side of the growth equation and credited to the consumption side, it follows that the volume of aggregate investment makes provision only for replacement (i.e. depreciation and obsolescence) and the net growth of investment. Consequently, also, the growth rate of investment makes provision only for replacement.

Hence, if μ is the depreciation ratio and α the obsolescence coefficient we have

$$r_i = (1 - \alpha)r_y = (\mu + \alpha)r_y$$

whence, $1 - \alpha = \mu + \alpha$

and   (i) $\mu + 2\alpha = 1$

           (ii) $\alpha = (1 - \mu)/2$

           (iii) $\mu = 1 - 2\alpha$

It follows, also, that $r_i = (1 - \alpha)r_y = (\mu + \alpha)r_y = \left(\dfrac{1 + \mu}{2}\right)r_y$. Thus the annual increase in investment is purely on account of the requirements of replacement, that is, to cover only depreciation and obsolescence, the net investment of the year being equal to the whole of the previous year's investment. The replacement coefficient in Type V is therefore always less than unity, the obsolescence or technological coefficient being always half the difference between unity and the depreciation coefficient. By implication, the depreciation coefficient is also always less than unity. These new conditions for Type V can be written as follows:

$$1 > \mu > 0$$
$$(1 - \mu)/2 = \alpha > 0$$

It is important to note, therefore, that, unlike Type III growth where the coefficient of replacement is unity, in Type V the coefficient of replacement is less than unity.

There remains for us to examine the changes that occur within a Type V economy as the value of α changes within the range $1 > \alpha > 0$, as μ also changes within the range $1 > \mu > 0$.

When $\mu = 0$, $\alpha = 0.5$, $r_i = 0.5\ r_y$ and
$$r_c = r_y(1+0.5\ I_0/C_0) = r_y(Y_0-0.5\ I_0)/C_0$$
We then have a Type V economy, in which there is no depreciation but only the retirement of obsolete equipment.

When $\mu = 1$, $\alpha = 0$, $r_i = r_y = r_c$
We then have the Harrod-Domar steady growth state (Type IV) in which no technological progress is possible, because there is no change in technology and no technological investment. All replacement is on account of depreciation.

Avoiding these two extreme situations in which, respectively, investment is not depreciated and where there is no technological progress, a Type V economy must have, or select, values for α such that $0.5 > \alpha > 0$, in order to retain its character and grow with a progressive technology. In the normal case, therefore, α will have a value less than 0.5, and the more it falls below this value the closer the value of μ approaches unity, while r_c approaches r_y asymptotically from a value above, and r_i approaches it from a value below, r_y. In general, as $\alpha \to 0$ we find also that $\mu \to 1$, and r_c and $r_i \to r_y$.

We may now write the investment programme for Type V as given by the formula
$$I_t = (1+r_i)^t I_0 = \left\{ 1+r_y(1-\alpha) \right\}^t I_0$$
Furthermore, since α cannot have a value equal to or exceeding 0.5, the value of r_i cannot fall as low as $0.5 r_y$ in a Type V economy, nor the value of r_c rise as high as $r_y(1+0.5\ I_0/C_0)$. These conditions constitute a set of consistency tests for the national accounts data in an economy with a Type V growth pattern.[8]

---

8. Some of the data in Tables I and II for the Type V patterns of various countries do not hold up under these tests, notably, those for Luxembourg, Canada, and Nigeria. It is possible, however, for the data relating to these countries to satisfy a different set of consistency tests for the case where $\mu > 1$. Such cases are, however, implicit cases of Type III growth. (See the subsequent discussion.)

As we shall see subsequently, the value $r_i = 0.5 \, r_y$ sets also the maximum value for the rate of population growth (or the rate of growth of the labour force) in a Type V economy, if investment per man is to continue growing and the society's capital stock should be regularly and effectively depreciated, while at the same time real income and consumption per capita increase.

(ii) $2 > \mu > 1$

We could change our assumption about the range of values for μ and admit values for it that are greater than unity. In this case α, the depreciation or technological coefficient will always be a positive quantity as must be the case in a technologically progressive economy. Then $\alpha = \mu - 1$.

This implies, if we accept a depreciation coefficient of a value greater than unity, that in a technologically progressive Type V economy the coefficient of depreciation μ is in excess of unity by the value of the technological coefficient α. And, as technological progress and innovation proceed, the greater becomes the value of the obsolescence or technological coefficient, and the greater, therefore, the depreciation coefficient. Also, as under the previous assumption, an increment of investment in any one year at the rate of r_i is required only in order to take care of replacement capital, provided that the net addition to society's capital stock made in that year is equal to the whole of the gross investment of the previous year.

Thus for Type V growth we may properly write the following equivalent expressions for the growth rate of investment r_i:

$$r_i = r_y(1 - \alpha) = r_y \left\{ 1 - (\mu - 1) \right\} = \left\{ 1 - (\mu - 1) \right\} \pi / r_y$$

where $\alpha = \mu - 1$, and $\pi = r_y^2$, as before.
But we may also write:

$$r_i = r_y(1 - \alpha) = r_y \left\{ (1 - 2\alpha) + \alpha \right\}$$

where, in the third equivalent expression, α is the obsolescence coefficient and $(1-2\alpha)$ the depreciation coefficient, both added together yielding the replacement coefficient of $(1-\alpha)$.

Hence, the two components of the actual growth rate of investment, $r_y(1-\alpha)$, are:

$r_y(1-2\alpha)$ for the growth rate of depreciation

and αr_y for the growth rate of obsolescence

Here, then are two apparently contradictory but very interesting results which are peculiar to the Type V growth pattern: on the one hand, the coefficient of potential and required depreciation μ is equal to $1+\alpha$, which with the obsolescence coefficient α yields a potential replacement coefficient of $1+2\alpha$, and a potential and required growth rate of $r_y(1+2\alpha)$ for aggregate investment (excluding incremental technological investment); on the other hand, the actual or realized depreciation coefficient α is equal to $1-2\alpha$, which with the obsolescence coefficient α gives a realized replacement coefficient of $1-\alpha$, and a realized growth rate of $r_y(1-\alpha)$ for aggregate investment (excluding incremental technological investment).

By comparison, therefore, we see that whereas for the Type III growth pattern the actual required growth rate of replacement capital is the same as that of aggregate output r_y, for the Type V growth pattern the actual growth rate of replacement capital is less than that of aggregate output, being equal to $r_y(1-\alpha)$, while the potential growth rate of replacement capital is higher than that of aggregate output and equal to $r_y(1+2\alpha)$. Thus for Type V potential depreciation is not only at a higher rate than actual depreciation — $r_y(1+\alpha)$ as compared to $r_y(1-2\alpha)$—but also at a higher rate than actual replacement—$r_y(1+\alpha)$ as compared to $r_y(1-\alpha)$.

The excess of the potential over the realized growth rate of depreciation is $3\alpha r_y$, the excess in terms of resources being $3\alpha r_y I_0$ in period 1; and the excess of the potential growth rate of depreciation over the realized growth rate of replacement is $2\alpha r_y$, the excess in terms of resources being $2\alpha r_y I_0$ in period 1. These discrepancies, however, cannot be satisfactorily explained within the framework of our investigation, namely, in terms of real resources at constant prices, since the sum total of available resources would already be accounted for by $\underline{Y}$ and its components, I and C. We need to proceed outside the framework of our discussion to find a plausible explanation. If, accordingly, we imported into the discussion current money values of the real resources available it becomes possible to argue that in a Type V economy funds currently set aside for depreciation considerably exceed the current value of the depreciation actually made, while the excess of depreciation funds over the value of the resources invested in replacement is two-thirds the excess over depreciation actually made.[9]

There are, of course, many possibilities of employment for the savings accumulated in the form of excess depreciation funds. They could be invested abroad, or in the domestic capital market in securities, used to augment technological investment, or just simply held as idle balances. If, however, a Type V economy were to invest all of its excess depreciation funds for this purpose, it would no longer continue in its growth pattern, but switch over to Type III. For then the new rate of growth of aggregate investment would be $r_i = r_y(1+2\alpha)$ and the new rate of growth of aggregate consumption will accordingly be $r_c = r_y(1-2\alpha I_0/C_0)$, yielding a Type III pattern in which marginal technological investment is twice the volume in its Type V

9. Evsey Domar's study on "Depreciation, Replacement and Growth", *The Economic Journal*, Vol. 63 1953, pp. 1-32 (reprinted as Essay VII in his *Essays in the Theory of Economic Growth*) arrived at results which showed that "in a growing society, replacement falls far short of depreciation" —"even with constant prices and correct depreciation charges (computed according to the straight-line method)." This conclusion would seem consonant with the explanation given above, even though Domar does not seem to include obsolescence in his definition of replacement. However, our explanation would be valid only for growth of the Type V pattern as the discrepancy between depreciation and replacement does not arise in Type III.

progenitor and $C_0 = 2 I_0$. Which perhaps shows that a Type V economy with accumulated depreciation funds could conceivably double its current marginal and total technological expenditures and increase its current replacement expenditures by three times as much as its current marginal technological expenditures.

Let us now examine the changes that occur within a Type V economy in which $\mu > 1$, as the value of α changes within the range $0 \leftrightarrow 1$. For this range of values of α, μ would have a value within the range of $1 \leftrightarrow 2$.

When $\alpha = 1$, $\mu = 2$, $r_i = 0$ and $r_c = r_y(1 + I_0/C_0)$
$$= r_y Y_0/C_0$$

We then have a Type VI economy, a limiting case of Type V in which r_i attains its minimum (non-negative) value and r_c its corresponding maximum value. But this pattern of growth, as we have seen, is incompatible with long-term growth.

When $\alpha = 0$, $\mu = 1$, $r_i = r_y = r_c$

We then have the Harrod-Domar steady-growth state (Type IV, a limiting case of Type V) in which technological progress, and therefore technological investment, is impossible (or indeterminate).

Avoiding these two extreme situations, this version of a Type V economy must have values of α such that $1 > \alpha > 0$, and consequently r_i must always be greater than zero but less than r_y, and r_c always less than $r_y(1+I_0/C_0)$ but greater than r_y

The constraints constitute a set of consistency tests for the national accounts data for a Type V economy in which $\mu > 1$. Comparing these tests with those for the case where $\mu < 1$ we may conclude that the condition $\mu > 1$ holds in a Type V economy where $r_y > r_i > 0$ and $r_y(1+I_0/C_0) > r_c > r_y(1+0.5\ I_0/C_0)$, and that accumulation of depreciation funds beyond actual depreciation effected is a feature of such economy. In which case the appropriate volume of depreciation funds could not be estimated in constant but in current prices, and, likewise, the potential volume of technological investment (both marginal and total) as well as the potential volume of replacement.

B. Summary: Investment Programme Required for
Each Main Type of Growth

It would be appropriate to summarize at this point the results that have been derived in the preceding discussion of investment requirements. In general, the investment programme has been found to contain three main elements: net investment, replacement (consisting of depreciation and obsolescence) and marginal technological investment. From this point on it is best to adopt the following symbols for these three elements.[10]

N = Net Investment (equals aggregate investment of the preceding period)
R = Replacement = $D + O$
D = Depreciation
O = Obsolescence
T = Aggregate Technological Investment
ΔT = Marginal Technological Investment

Thus we have seen that for Type III

$$I_1 = N_1 + R_1 + (\Delta T)_1$$

and that for Type V

$$I_1 = N_1 + R_1$$

We should now study these results a little further.

(a) *Type III*

The investment programme was found to be given by

$$I_t = \left\{ 1 + r_y(1 + \alpha C_0/I_0) \right\}^t I_0 \qquad (14.1)$$

---

10. These symbols are straightforward and simple, although there may be a little inconvenience with regard to T which was used in my earlier article, for net investment as mentioned in the introduction to this chapter. However, the replacement of T by N for net investment and the confining of T to technological investment has mnemonic advantages which soon outweigh any initial inconvenience.

which may be written, alternatively, as

$$I_t = \left\{ 1 + r_y (1 + \alpha C_0/I_0) \right\} I_{t-1}$$

where $N_t = I_{t-1}$, $R_t = r_y I_{t-1}$, $D_t = r_y(1 - \alpha C_0/I_0)I_{t-1}$,

$$O_t = \alpha r_y \frac{C_0}{I_0} I_{t-1} = (\Delta T)_t$$

and the depreciation coefficient and the obsolescence or technological coefficient, as before, are respectively $\mu = 1 - \alpha C_0/I_0$ and $1 - \mu = \alpha C_0/I_0$. It was demonstrated that the marginal technological investment (equivalent to obsolescence) was already extracted from aggregate consumption and fully included, from the outset, in aggregate investment.

(b) *Type V*

In this case the investment programme is given by

$$I_t = \left\{ 1 + r_y(1 - \alpha) \right\}^t I_0 \qquad (14.2)$$

or

$$I_t = \left\{ 1 + r_y(1 - \alpha) \right\} I_{t-1}$$

The growth of investment provides only for replacement, marginal technological investment having been already deducted and included as a component of aggregate consumption. Thus the aggregate investment programme excludes marginal technological investment, consisting only of N_t and $R_t (= D_t + O_t)$,

For $1 > \mu > 0$

$$N_t = I_{t-1}, \quad R_t = r_y(1 - \alpha)I_{t-1}, \quad D_t = r_y(1 - 2\alpha)I_{t-1},$$

$$O_t = \alpha r_y I_{t-1}$$

and the depreciation and obsolescence coefficients are, respectively

$$\mu = 1 - 2\alpha, \text{ and } \alpha = (1 - \mu)/2.$$

For the case where $2 > \mu > 1$,

$$N_t = I_{t-1}, \quad R_t = r_y(1 + 2\alpha)I_{t-1}, \quad D_t = r_y(1 + \alpha)I_{t-1} \quad \text{and}$$

$$O_t = \alpha r_y I_{t-1}$$

where the depreciation and obsolescence coefficients are, respectively, $\mu = 1 + \alpha$, and $\alpha = \mu - 1$. This case was found to be effectively a Type III if the accumulated depreciation funds, which resulted in a depreciation coefficient greater than unity, were all effectively invested for this purpose. For this case, then, matters would roughly parallel the situation in Type III.

If the investment programme for Type V is to include marginal technological investment *in a given period t*, then using the symbols

$$\dot{I}_t = \text{Aggregate investment including } (\Delta T)_t$$

$$I_{.t} = \text{Aggregate investment excluding } (\Delta T)_t$$

we find that

$$\dot{I}_t = I_t + (\Delta T)_t = \left\{1 + r_y(1 - \alpha)\right\} I_{t-1} + \alpha r_y I_{t-1}$$

so that $\dot{I}_t = (1 + r_y)I_{t-1} = I_0(1 + r_y)(1 + r_i)^{t-1}$ (14.2.1)

Then $I_{.t} = I_0(1 + r_i)^{t-1}$ (14.2.2)

Since $I_{.0} = I_0 < \dot{I}_0$, and $r_i < r_y$, it follows that

$$\dot{I}_t = I_0(1 + r_y)(1 + r_i)^{t-1} < \dot{I}_0(1 + r_y)^t$$

Similarly, aggregate consumption including ΔT may be represented by $\dot{C} = C$, and aggregate consumption excluding ΔT by $\underset{.}{C}$, so that

$$\dot{C}_t = C_t = C_0(1 + r_c)^t \tag{14.2.3}$$

and

$$\underset{.}{C}_t = C_t - (\Delta T)_t = (1 + r_y)C_{t-1} > \underset{.}{C}_0(1 + r_y)^t \tag{14.2.4}$$

However, if, *from the outset*, incremental technological investment was included in aggregate investment and deducted from aggregate consumption, then the investment programme for Type V would be:

$$\dot{I}_t = \dot{I}_0(1 + r_y)^t \tag{14.2.5}$$

and the consumption programme,

$$\underset{.}{C}_t = \underset{.}{C}_0(1 + r_y)^t \tag{14.2.6}$$

with both aggregate investment and aggregate consumption growing at the same rate as aggregate income, namely, r_y.

Furthermore, it can be easily demonstrated that while $\underset{.}{I}_0(1+r_y)(1+r_i)^{t-1} < \dot{I}_0(1+r_y)^t$ and $\dot{C}_0(1+r_y)(1+r_c)^{t-1}$

$> \underset{.}{C}_0(1+r_y)^t$, it is nevertheless true that $Y_0(1 + r_y)^t$

$= \dot{C}_0(1+r_y)(1+r_c)^{t-1} + \underset{.}{I}_0(1+r_y)(1+r_i)^{t-1} = \underset{.}{C}_0(1+r_y)^t$

$$+ \dot{I}_0(1+r_y)^t$$

Thus, while steady growth does not occur in practice, by suitable manipulation, that is by including incremental technological investment in aggregate investment *from the outset*, a Type V pattern can be transformed into a formal pattern of steady growth. Yet, even in this case, technology is not unchanged and technological investment continues to grow, but both incremental and total technological investment are indeterminate and the misleading impression results that all replacement is on account of depreciation, and that the incremental and aggregate capital-output ratios are both equal and constant.

C. Technological Investment Required for Each
Main Type of Growth

The magnitude of required marginal technological investment in any period is always given by the formulae:

$$(\Delta T)_t = \alpha r_y \frac{C_0}{I_0} I_{t-1} \quad = \alpha r_y (1+r_i)^{t-1} C_0 = O_t \quad \text{(Type III)}$$

$$(\Delta T)_t = \alpha r_y I_{t-1} \quad = \alpha r_y (1+r_i)^{t-1} I_0 = O_t \quad \text{(Type V)}$$

In order to determine the total technological investment required in any given period, we need to take account of the fact that technological investment is a part of aggregate investment and must therefore grow at the same rate as aggregate investment. Aggregate investment must therefore always be defined to include marginal technological investment. To the extent that the national accounts of a country exclude any part of technological investment from aggregate investment for any reason whatsoever (for example, for military or strategic reasons) both the gross product and the gross investment of the country would be understated and, consequently, the required volume of aggregate technological investment. Nevertheless, for the figures of gross product and investment reported in the accounts, the required volume of aggregate technological investment appropriate to the particular levels and rates of growth of aggregate output and investment (as reported) would be substantially correct—provided, of course, the national accounts data satisfy the particular set of consistency tests applicable to the given pattern of growth.

That aggregate technological investment grows at the same rate as aggregate investment presents no problem for Type III since technological investment is automatically included in aggregate investment, and its rate of growth is therefore the rate of growth of aggregate investment. For Type V, however, the position is somewhat different, since incremental technological investment is excluded from incremental investment. Hence it follows that total technological investment is only partially included in aggregate investment, as given by the investment formula for Type V, unless aggregate investment is first defined to include marginal technological investment. In the latter case, Equation 14.2.5 rather than Equation 14.2.2 would be the appropriate formula to use. Alternatively, since incremental technological investment is automatically included in incremental consumption in Type V, it follows that the magnitude of aggregate technological investment can be derived directly from the formula for aggregate consumption (including technological investment).[11] In both Types III and V aggregate investment, including total technological investment, grows at the rate of r_y and aggregate technological investment must therefore grow at this same rate.

Required Aggregate Technological Investment for Type III Growth

Given that technological investment is included in aggregate investment and must therefore grow at the same rate as aggregate investment, namely r_i, it follows that

$$(\Delta T)_t / T_{t-1} = r_i$$

so that $T_{t-1} = (\Delta T)_t / r_i$

and $T_t = T_{t-1} + \Delta T_{t-1} = T_{t-1} + (\Delta T)_t$

Since $(\Delta T)_t = \alpha r_y \dfrac{C_0}{I_0} I_{t-1}$

---

11. It is necessary to add the words in parentheses in order to avoid any possible mistake or confusion, in view of Equation 14.2.6 which gives the volume of aggregate consumption excluding technological investment.

we have $T_{t-1} = \dfrac{\alpha r_y}{r_i} \dfrac{C_0}{I_0} I_{t-1} = \dfrac{\alpha r_y C_0}{r_i} (1+r_i)^{t-1}$

$= \left(\dfrac{r_i - r_c}{r_y}\right) \dfrac{r_y I_0 C_0}{r_i I_0 Y_0} I_{t-1} = \left(\dfrac{r_i - r_c}{r_i}\right) \dfrac{C_0}{Y_0} I_{t-1}$

and $T_t = \alpha r_y \left(1 + \dfrac{1}{r_i}\right) \dfrac{C_0}{I_0} I_{t-1} = (r_i - r_c)\left(\dfrac{1 + r_i}{r_i}\right) \dfrac{C_0}{Y_0} I_{t-1}$

$= \dfrac{1+r_i}{r_i} (\Delta T)_t$

These formulae measure the corresponding magnitudes of replacement, marginal and aggregate, on account of obsolescence which *should have been made* by the end of period t since the base period. With technological investment, however, such investment activity is *repetitive*, not *cumulative* as in the case of replacement on account of obsolescence or of depreciation, because in every period the total investment of the preceding period is repeated as net investment, and of this net investment technological investment is *always* a part. Moreover, an addition to previous total technological investment is always made in the current period as an element of the increment in gross investment of the current period. (These observations also apply to Type V growth.)

The contribution of aggregate technological investment to aggregate output, for any given period t, is given by the ratio of aggregate technological investment to aggregate investment in that period. Since, however, aggregate technological investment grows at the same rate as aggregate investment, the contribution of marginal technological investment to marginal output is always the same as the contribution of aggregate technological investment to aggregate output.

Hence,

$$
\begin{Bmatrix}
\text{Contribution of Aggregate} \\
\text{Technological Investment} \\
\text{to Aggregate Output}
\end{Bmatrix}
=
\begin{Bmatrix}
\text{Contribution of Marginal} \\
\text{Technological Investment} \\
\text{to Marginal Output}
\end{Bmatrix}
$$

$$
= \frac{T_t}{I_t} = \frac{(\Delta T)_t}{(\Delta I)_t} = \frac{\alpha r_y C_0}{r_i I_0}
$$

But $\dfrac{\alpha r_y C_0}{r_i I_0} = \left(\dfrac{r_i - r_c}{r_i}\right)\dfrac{C_0}{Y_0}$ (where $\alpha C_0/I_0 = \left(\dfrac{r_i - r_c}{r_y}\right)\dfrac{C_0}{Y_0}$

$$\text{= Coefficient of Technological Investment)}$$

Hence, $\begin{pmatrix}\text{Contribution of Technological} \\ \text{Investment to Aggregate Output}\end{pmatrix} = \left(\dfrac{r_i - r_c}{r_i}\right)\dfrac{C_0}{Y_0}$

$$
= \frac{r_y}{r_i} \text{ x Coefficient of Technological Invest-}\text{ment}
$$

Required Aggregate Technological Investment for
Type V Growth

The volume of aggregate investment including marginal technological investment, in any period t, is given by $(1+r_y)^t I_0$, and its growth rate is r_y, the same as that of technological investment. Consequently,

$$(\Delta T)_t / T_{t-1} = r_y$$

so that $\quad T_{t-1} = (\Delta T)_t / r_y$

and $\quad T_t = T_{t-1} + \Delta T_{t-1} = T_{t-1} + (\Delta T)_t$

Since $\quad (\Delta T)_t = \alpha r_y I_{t-1}$

we have $\quad T_{t-1} = \alpha I_{t-1} = \left(\dfrac{r_c - r_i}{r_y}\right)\dfrac{C_0}{Y_0} I_{t-1}$

and
$$T_t = \alpha(1+r_y)I_{t-1} = \left(\frac{r_c - r_i}{r_y}\right)(1+r_y)\frac{C_0}{Y_0}I_{t-1}$$
$$= \frac{1+r_y}{r_y}(\Delta T)_t$$

As in Type III, these formulae measure the corresponding magnitudes of replacement, marginal and aggregate, on account of obsolescence which should have been made by the end of period t since the base period.

Again, as in Type III, the contribution of aggregate technological investment to aggregate output, for any given period t, is given by the ratio of aggregate technological investment to aggregate investment in that period. Since, however, aggregate technological investment grows at the same rate as aggregate investment, the contribution of marginal technological investment to marginal output is always the same as the contribution of aggregate technological investment to aggregate output. Hence,

$$\left.\begin{array}{l}\text{Contribution of Aggregate}\\ \text{Technological Investment}\\ \text{to Aggregate Output}\end{array}\right\} = \left\{\begin{array}{l}\text{Contribution of Marginal}\\ \text{Technological Investment}\\ \text{to Marginal Output}\end{array}\right.$$

$$= \frac{T_t}{\dot{I}_t} = \frac{(\Delta T)_t}{(\Delta \dot{I})_t} = \alpha$$

But $\alpha = \left(\dfrac{r_c - r_i}{r_y}\right)\dfrac{C_0}{Y_0}$ = Coefficient of Technological

Investment

Hence, $\left.\begin{array}{l}\text{Contribution of Technological}\\ \text{Investment to Aggregate Output}\end{array}\right\} = \left\{\begin{array}{l}\text{Coefficient of}\\ \text{Technological}\\ \text{Investment}\end{array}\right.$

D.   Limits of the Growth Rates of Investment and
     Consumption for the Two Main Patterns of Growth

The curves we obtained in Figures I and II, we may recall, are essentially timeless curves showing the variations in r_y, r_i, and r_c as α assumes different values which, for the purpose of plotting, were assumed to vary with time, an assumption which is not really necessary. Removing the assumption of time we should obtain the same result by plotting r_y, r_i, and r_c directly against various values of α. Thus the relevant parts of the curve are those between $\alpha = 0$ and $\alpha = 1$.

We may now set down schematically the maximum and minimum values of r_i and r_c possible under the two main patterns of growth, as specified previously and illustrated by the blocked sections of Figures I and II. At the same time it should be understood that these maxima and minima should be avoided if the normal patterns of growth should be maintained at positive values for the obsolescence and depreciation coefficients.

Type III: $1 > \mu > 0,\ I_0/C_0 > \alpha > 0$

$r_y Y_0/I_0 > r_i > 0$:

$\qquad r_i \text{ (max)} = 2 r_y \qquad\qquad (\alpha = I_0/C_0,\ \ \mu = 0)$

$\qquad r_i \text{ (min)} = \ \ r_y \qquad\qquad (\alpha = 0, \qquad \mu = 1)$

$r_y > r_c > 0$:

$\qquad r_c \text{ (max)} = \ \ r_y \qquad\qquad (\alpha = 0, \qquad \mu = 1)$

$\qquad r_c \text{ (min)} = \ \ r_y\,(1 - I_0/C_0) \quad (\alpha = I_0/C_0,\ \ \mu = 0)$

Type V (i): $1 > \mu > 0,\ 0.5 > \alpha > 0$

$r_y > r_i > 0$:

$\qquad r_i \text{ (max)} = \ \ r_y \qquad\qquad (\alpha = 0, \quad \mu = 1)$

$\qquad r_i \text{ (min)} = 0.5\,r_y \qquad\quad (\alpha = 0.5,\ \mu = 0)$

$$r_y Y_0 / C_0 > r_c > r_y:$$

$$r_c \text{ (max)} = r_y (1 + 0.5\ I_0 / C_0) \quad (\alpha = 0.5,\ \mu = 0)$$

$$r_c \text{ (min)} = r_y \quad\quad\quad\quad\quad (\alpha = 0,\ \quad \mu = 1)$$

Type V (ii): $\quad 2 > \mu > 1,\ 1 > \alpha > 0$

$$r_y > r_i > 0$$

$$r_i \text{ (max)} = r_y \quad\quad\quad\quad\quad (\alpha = 0,\ \quad \mu = 2)$$

$$r_i \text{ (min)} = 0 \quad\quad\quad\quad\quad (\alpha = 1,\ \quad \mu = 2)$$

$$r_y Y_0 / C_0 > r_c > r_y:$$

$$r_c \text{ (max)} = r_y (1 + I_0 / C_0) = r_y Y_0 / C_0 \quad (\alpha = 1,\ \mu = 2)$$

$$r_c \text{ (min)} = r_y \quad\quad\quad\quad\quad (\alpha = 0,\ \quad \mu = 1)$$

E.   Inversion of Types III and V

We have seen that Types III and V are images of each other with respect to the line of steady-growth.[12] Moreover, they are exact images, taking into account the constraints relevant to each type.

The inversion of a normal Type III economy $(1 > \mu > 0,\ I_0 / C_0 > \alpha > 0)$ about the line of steady-growth produces an image corresponding to a Type V subject to the conditions: $2 > \mu > 1$, and $1 > \alpha > 0$.

By contrast, the inversion of a Type V economy subject to the conditions $1 > \mu > 0$ and $0.5 > \alpha > 0$ produces a special kind of Type III subject to the conditions $1 > \mu > 0.5$ and $0.5\ I_0 / C_0 > \alpha > 0$.

---

12. See Chapter II, section on Growth Rate Curves

The inversion of a Type V economy subject to the conditions $2 > \mu > 1$ and $1 > \alpha > 0$ yields a normal Type III subject to the conditions $1 > \mu > 0$ and $I_0/C_0 > \alpha > 0$.

These results are schematically summarized below:

Inversion of:

Type III: $1 > \mu > 0$, $I_0/C_0 > \alpha > 0$

$r_i(\max) = 2r_y$ $(\alpha = I_0/C_0, \mu = 0)$

$r_i(\min) = r_y$ $(\alpha = 0 \quad, \mu = 1)$

$r_c(\max) = r_y$ $(\alpha = 0 \quad, \mu = 1)$

$r_c(\min) = r_y(1-I_0/C_0)$ $(\alpha = I_0/C_0, \mu = 0)$

Type V(i): $1 > \mu > 0$, $0.5 > \alpha > 0$

$r_i(\max) = r_y$ $(\alpha = 0, \mu = 1)$

$r_i(\min) = 0.5\ r_y$ $(\alpha = 0.5, \mu = 0)$

$r_c(\max) = r_y(1+0.5\ I_0/C_0)$ $(\alpha = 0.5, \mu = 0)$

$r_c(\min) = r_y$ $(\alpha = 0, \mu = 1)$

Type V(ii): $2 > \mu > 1$, $1 > \alpha > 0$

$r_i(\max) = r_y$ $(\alpha = 0, \mu = 1)$

$r_i(\min) = 0$ $(\alpha = 1, \mu = 2)$

$r_c(\max) = r_y(1+I_0/C_0) = r_y Y_0/C_0 (\alpha = 1, \mu = 2)$

$r_c(\min) = r_y$ $(\alpha = 0, \mu = 1)$

Yields:

Type V: $2 > \mu > 1$, $1 > \alpha > 0$

$r_i(\max) = r_y$ $(\alpha = 0, \mu = 1)$

$r_i(\min) = 0$ $(\alpha = 1, \mu = 2)$

$r_c(\max) = r_y(1+I_0/C_0)$ $(\alpha = 1, \mu = 2)$

$r_c(\min) = r_y$ $(\alpha = 1, \mu = 1)$

Type III (special): $1 > \mu > 0.5$, $0.5 I_0/C_0 > \alpha > 0$

$r_i(\max) = r_y(1+0.5)$ $(\alpha = 0.5 I_0/C_0, \mu = 0.5)$

$r_i(\min) = r_y$ $(\alpha = 0 \quad, \mu = 1)$

$r_c(\max) = r_y$ $(\alpha = 0 \quad, \mu = 1)$

$r_c(\min) = r_y(1-0.5 I_0/C_0)$ $(\alpha = 0.5 I_0/C_0, \mu = 0.5)$

Type III (normal): $1 > \mu > 0$, $I_0/C_0 > \alpha > 0$

$r_i(\max) = 2r_y$ $(\alpha = I_0/C_0, \mu = 0)$

$r_i(\min) = r_y$ $(\alpha = 0 \quad, \mu = 1)$

$r_c(\max) = r_y$ $(\alpha = 0 \quad, \mu = 1)$

$r_c(\min) = r_y(1-I_0/C_0)$ $(\alpha = I_0/C_0, \mu = 0)$

F. Population and the Patterns of Economic Growth

It is not enough merely to consider the patterns of absolute growth of aggregate output, consumption, and investment, for these do not take on significance until related to the rate of population growth. For economic development means, if anything, a sustained increase in per capita real income, consumption, and investment, which together constitute the real content of the level of living. Accordingly, it is necessary to consider in addition the required rates of population growth which should make an all round improvement in the level of living become a reality.

We are here considering the three elements, per capita income, consumption, and investment together, rather than per capita income alone—which is the conventional approach and valid only for Type IV which requires that $r_p < r_y$. For per capita income alone, even in net terms, is not a sufficient determinant of the real living standard or its content unless we consider at the same time what is happening to per capita consumption and per capita investment. This is especially important, considering that it is often quite possible for per capita gross or net income to increase while per capita consumption or per capita investment declines. It is only when gross or net per capita income, as well as gross or net per capita consumption and gross or net per capita investment, increases that we are entitled to declare that real living standards have increased.

It follows, therefore, that it is the slowest growing of the three magnitudes (real income, consumption, and investment) rather than the rate of growth of aggregate real income that is relevant to determining both the appropriate rate of population growth and the real content of the standard of living. This means consumption in Type III, and investment in Type V. Thus aggregate real income is itself not a primary, but a secondary and dependent, criterion of the content of living—unless where we are dealing with the rather special theoretical case of Type IV.

Appropriate Rate of Population Growth for Type III

For Type III we have to consider r_c in relation to r_p. We have seen that the r_c (min) condition

$$r_c = r_y(1 - I_0/C_0)$$

involves a failure to meet required depreciation of the capital stock, while the occurence of

$$r_p = r_c$$

implies no growth in net consumption. We should therefore aim at preventing these two conditions from occurring in Type III. Hence, taking the two conditions together,

$$r_p = r_c = r_y(1 - I_0/C_0)$$

defines the asymptotic values of r_c (minimum) and r_p (maximum), so that we should always have

$$r_c > r_y(1-I_0/C_0) \geqq r_p$$

This implies that

$$r_w \gtreqless r_y I_0/C_0$$

For practical purposes we may work with the maximum value of r_p and the minimum value of r_w. Hence, the appropriate values of r_p and r_w for Type III are given by

$$r_p = r_y(1-I_0/C_0)$$
$$r_w = r_y I_0/C_0$$

Given, therefore, the base year values of Y, C, I, and their respective rates of growth we may summarize below the appropriate growth rates of the real components of the standard of living in Type III:

Required:

Rate of Growth of Gross Income per capita =

$$r_{(Y/P)} = \frac{r_y - r_p}{1 + r_p} = \frac{r_y I_0/C_0}{1 + r_y(1-I_0/C_0)}$$

Rate of growth of Gross Consumption per capita =

$$r_{(C/P)} = \frac{r_c - r_p}{1 + r_p} = \frac{r_y(I_0/C_0 - \alpha)}{1 + r_y(1-I_0/C_0)}$$

Rate of growth of Gross Investment per capita =

$$r_{(I/P)} = \frac{r_i - r_p}{1 + r_p} = \frac{r_y(\alpha C_0/I_0 + I_0/C_0)}{1 + r_y(1-I_0/C_0)}$$

$$\text{where } I_0/C_0 > \alpha > 0$$

Appropriate Rate of Population Growth for Type V

For Type V we have to consider r_i in relation to r_p. The two versions of Type V need to be considered separately according as

      (i) $1 > \mu > 0,\ 0.5 > \alpha > 0$

or

      (ii) $2 > \mu > 1,\ 1 > \alpha > 0$

(i) $1 > \mu > 0,\ 0.5 > \alpha > 0$:

The condition $r_i = 0.5\ r_y$, as we have seen, involves a failure to depreciate the capital stock as required, while the condition $r_p = r_i$ puts a check to the growth of investment per capita. Thus we must in this version of Type V avoid the conditions

$$r_p = r_i = 0.5 r_y$$

which define the asymptotic values of r_i (minimum) and r_p (maximum). Hence we must always ensure that

$$r_i > 0.5 r_y > r_p$$

which implies, also, that

$$r_w \geqq 0.5 r_y$$

In practice, we would need to operate with the maximum value of r_p and the minimum value of r_w, which would give the appropriate values or r_p and r_w as follows:

$$r_p = 0.5 r_y = r_w$$

Given the base year values of Y, C, I, and their respective growth rates we summarize below the appropriate rates of growth of the real components of the standard of living for this version of Type V.

Required:

Rate of growth of Gross Income per capita

$$= r_{(Y/P)} = \frac{r_y - r_p}{1 + r_p} = \frac{0.5 r_y}{1 + 0.5 r_y}$$

Rate of growth of Gross Consumption per capita

$$= r_{(C/P)} = \frac{r_c - r_p}{1 + r_p} = \frac{r_y(0.5 + \alpha\, I_0/C_0)}{1 + 0.5\, r_y}$$

Rate of growth of Gross Investment per capita

$$= r_{(I/P)} = \frac{r_i - r_p}{1 + r_p} = \frac{r_y(0.5 - \alpha)}{1 + 0.5 r_y}$$

where $0.5 > \alpha > 0$

(ii) $2 > \mu > 1, \quad 1 > \alpha > 0$:

For this version of Type V, the condition $r_i = 0$ puts a stop to the growth of investment, while the condition $r_p = r_i$ checks the growth of investment per capita. So that the asymptotic values of r_i (minimum) and r_p (maximum) must be avoided, namely,

$$r_p = r_i = 0$$

in favour of $r_i > 0 \geqq r_p$.

For practical purposes of positive growth, however, r_p cannot be zero or negative as we should then have spurious growth per capita with a stationary or declining population. Hence $\Delta P \leqq 0$ is always ruled out from the definition of growth. We must find more satisfactory inequality relations for r_i and r_p, which we can do by reflecting on the properties of the inversion of the two main types of growth.

This version of Type V is the image of a normal Type III $(1 > \mu > 0)$, so that consumption which, before the inversion of Type III, was the slowest growing magnitude becomes, after inversion, the fastest growing. Investment, after the inversion, plays the growth role of consumption before the inversion. Appropriately, therefore, we may use the asymptotic limit of consumption in an uninverted Type III as the asymptotic limit of investment in the inverted Type III (i.e., the version of Type V under consideration). Hence, the task of an economy conforming to the present version of Type V would be to ensure always that,

$$r_i > r_y(1-I_0/C_0) \geqq r_p$$

a condition which ensures that

$$r_w \geqq r_y I_0/C_0$$

As before, we work with the maximum value of r_p and the minimum value of r_w.

Given the base year values of Y, C, I, and their respective rates of growth we may summarize the appropriate growth rates of the real components of the standard of living of this version of Type V.

Required:

Rate of growth of Gross Income per capita

$$= r_{(Y/P)} = \frac{r_y - r_p}{1 + r_p} = \frac{r_y I_0/C_0}{1 + r_y(1-I_0/C_0)}$$

Rate of growth of Gross Consumption per capita

$$= r_{(C/P)} = \frac{r_c - r_p}{1 + r_p} = \frac{r_y I_0/C_0(1 + \alpha)}{1 + r_y(1-I_0/C_0)}$$

Rate of growth of Gross Investment per capita

$$= r_{(I/P)} = \frac{r_i - r_p}{1 + r_p} = \frac{r_y(I_0/C_0 - \alpha)}{1 + r_y(1-I_0/C_0)}$$

where $1 > \alpha > 0$

Appropriate Rate of Population Growth for Type V
Formally Transformed into Type IV

The inclusion of marginal technological investment from the outset in aggregate investment makes it possible to "formalize" a Type V into a Type IV in which all rates of growth are constant and equal to r_y. The question of a minimum value for r_i does not therefore arise, and all that is required is that r_p be less than r_y—by how much, it is impossible to say. The appropriate r_p becomes indeterminate and all values of r_p less than r_y are then admissible. Hence, this indeterminacy of Type IV makes all discussions vague concerning matters that should otherwise be specific, the discussion being conducted in terms of "more than" or "less than". This is an additional aspect of the steady-growth model which makes it unsuitable for a determinate planning of appropriate and specific rates of growth of the real components of the standard of living. We can only proceed by adopting arbitrary values for r_p and r_w, subject to the condition that $r_y = r_p + r_w$. Accordingly, the summary of the appropriate growth rates of the real components of the standard of living would be as follows:

Required:

Rate of growth of Gross Income per capita $\left\{ r_{(Y/P)} \right\}$

= Rate of growth of Gross Consumption per capita

$\left\{ r_{(C/P)} \right\}$

= Rate of growth of Gross Investment per capita

$\left\{ r_{(I/P)} \right\}$

$$= \frac{r_y - r_p}{1 + r_p}$$

All gross rates are equal—an apparently simple task for the planner but a most difficult, if not possible, one to execute.

G.   Policy Implications

Our discussion of the characteristics and inversion of the two main growth patterns indicates the possibility of one and the same economy exhibiting either one or the other pattern of growth at different periods in its evolution. The discussion also indicates further policy and other implications. First, it implies the possibility of growth without fluctuations under either pattern, contrary to the widely held belief in some quarters that growth is possible only through fluctuations.

Second, on the policy level, it implies that the usual prescription of keeping the rate of growth of population below the growth rate of aggregate output in order to secure an increase in per capita income and real living standards is not only vague and inadequate but also only relevant to a Type IV growth pattern, hence of not much use to planners. The question by how much should the growth rate of population be kept below the growth rate of total output is left indeterminate.

The conventional prescription for population policy with regard to output growth is inadequate in regard to ensuring a simultaneous increase in the three main elements of the real standard of living, namely income, consumption, and investment, in those cases of growth that really matter, that is to say, cases conforming to Types III and V. As we have seen already (Section F), population growth rate should appropriately be controlled in regard to the growth rate of consumption in Type III and to the growth rate of investment in Type V. For, unless this is done, merely regulating the growth of population with regard to the growth rate of aggregate output could result in a decline in per capita real consumption in Type III and in per capita investment in Type V. Continuous growth is ensured, as in the developed countries of Europe, North America, and Japan, by keeping the growth rate of population below those of consumption and investment —in addition, of course, to continued technological progress.

Third, and still on the policy level, certain prescriptions are implied in regard also to policy in relation to depreciation, obsolescence, and technological investment, as concerns the values of the relevant coefficients.

A summary of the principal policy prescription follows:

Type III

(a) *Demographic Policy*:

$$r_c > r_y(1-I_0/C_0) \gtreqless r_p$$

(b) *Consumption and Investment*:

$$r_y > r_c > r_y(1-I_0/C_0)$$

$$2r_y > r_i > r_y$$

(c) *Depreciation, Obsolescence and Technological Investment*:

$$1 > \mu = 1-\alpha C_0/I_0 > 0$$

$$I_0/C_0 > \alpha = (r_i-r_c)I_0/r_y Y_0 > 0$$

Type V

(i)   (ii)

(a) *Demographic Policy*:

$$r_i > 0.5r_y \gtreqless r_p \qquad\qquad r_i > r_y(1-I_0/C_0) \gtreqless r_p$$

(b) *Consumption and Investment*:

$$r_y(1+0.5I_0/C_0) > r_c > r_y \qquad r_y(1+I_0/C_0) > r_c > r_y$$

$$r_y > r_i > 0.5r_y \qquad\qquad r_y > r_i > r_y(1-I_0/C_0$$

(c) *Depreciation, Obsolescence and Technological Investment*:

$$1 > \mu = 1-2\alpha > 0 \qquad\qquad 2 > \mu = 1+\alpha > 1$$

$$0.5 > \alpha = (r_c-r_i)C_0/r_y Y_0 > 0 \qquad 1 > \alpha = (r_c-r_i)C_0/r_y Y_0 > 0$$

H. Behaviour of the Investment Coefficient over
    Time in the Different Patterns of Growth

The growth of investment over time carries implications for the investment coefficient, that is, investment as a percentage of (real) gross domestic
(or available) product. It is necessary, therefore, to
inquire into the behaviour of this ratio over time, as
growth proceeds.

The investment coefficient in period t is given
by the relation

$$\left(\frac{I}{Y}\right)_t = \dot{\sigma}_t = \left(\frac{1+r_i}{1+r_y}\right)^t \frac{I_0}{Y_0} \tag{15}$$

where investment and the savings to finance it are
assumed always equal in fact, both from a resource
point of view as well as ex post; so that the investment
coefficient is equivalent to the saving coefficient, $\dot{\sigma}_t$,
both measured in gross real terms.

According as we are dealing with growth of Type
III, IV, or V, $r_i \gtreqless r_y$, and the respective rates of growth
of investment are:

$$r_y(1+\alpha C_0/I_0), \; r_y, \; \text{and} \; r_y \, (1-\alpha)$$

Under these conditions equation 15 becomes

$$\left(\frac{I}{Y}\right)_t = \dot{\sigma}_t = \frac{I_0}{Y_0}\left(1+\frac{\alpha r_y C_0/I_0}{1+r_y}\right)^t$$

$$= \dot{\sigma}_0\left(1+\frac{\alpha r_y C_0/I_0}{1+r_y}\right)^t \tag{15.1 (Type III)}$$

$$\text{or} \left(\frac{I}{Y}\right)_t = \dot{\sigma}_t = \frac{I_0}{Y_0} = \dot{\sigma}_0 \tag{15.2 (Type IV)}$$

$$\text{or} \left(\frac{I}{Y}\right)_t = \dot{\sigma}_t = \frac{I_0}{Y_0}\left(1 - \frac{\alpha r_y}{1 + r_y}\right)^t$$

$$= \dot{\sigma}_0 \left(1 - \frac{\alpha r_y}{1 + r_y}\right)^t \qquad (15.3) \text{ Type V}$$

Thus the rates of growth of $\left(\frac{I}{Y}\right)_t$ or $\dot{\sigma}_t$ are respectively

$$r_{(I/Y)_t} = r_{\dot{\sigma}_t} = \frac{\alpha r_y C_0/I_0}{1 + r_y} \qquad (\text{Type III})$$

$$r_{(I/Y)_t} = r_{\dot{\sigma}_t} = 0 \qquad (\text{Type IV})$$

$$r_{(I/Y)_t} = r_{\dot{\sigma}_t} = \frac{-\alpha r_y}{1 + r_y} \qquad (\text{Type V})$$

These results indicate that in a Type III economy the savings-investment coefficient will tend to increase over time, remain constant under steady growth, and diminish in a Type V economy. (With the transformation of the growth equation for Type V into one for Type IV, the savings-investment ratio will remain constant over time).

By implication, the marginal propensity to save will increase over time in a Type III economy, remain constant in a Type IV economy (as well as in a Type V economy formally transformed into a Type IV), and decline in a Type V economy.

I. Behaviour of the Marginal Propensity to Save over
   Time in the Different Patterns of Growth

The marginal propensity to save, being defined as $\left(\frac{\Delta S}{\Delta Y}\right)_t$, or $\left(\frac{\Delta I}{\Delta Y}\right)_t$ since we assume for planning purposes and for growth that savings and investment are identical, is derived generally from the following formula:

$$\left(\frac{\Delta S}{\Delta Y}\right)_t = \frac{\Delta I_{t-1}}{\Delta Y_{t-1}} = \frac{r_i}{r_y}\left(\frac{1+r_i}{1+r_y}\right)^{t-1}\frac{I_0}{Y_0} \tag{15.a}$$

This becomes, for the different patterns of growth

$$\left(\frac{\Delta S}{\Delta Y}\right)_t = (1+\alpha C_0/I_0)\left(1+\frac{\alpha r_y C_0/I_0}{1+r_y}\right)^{t-1}\frac{I_0}{Y_0} \tag{15.a.1}$$
(Type III)

or $\left(\frac{\Delta S}{\Delta Y}\right)_t = \frac{I_0}{Y_0}$ (15.a.2) (Type IV)

or $\left(\frac{\Delta S}{\Delta Y}\right)_t = (1-\alpha)\left(1-\frac{\alpha r_y}{1+r_y}\right)^{t-1}\frac{I_0}{Y_0}$ (15.a.3) (Type V)

Thus the rate of growth of the marginal and average propensity to save are the same in a given type of growth. This rate is positive, zero, or negative in Types III, IV, and V respectively, indicating that the coefficient of the marginal, like the average, propensity to save must increase in Type III and decrease in Type V, over time, remaining constant in Type IV.

These results represent an important qualification to Keynesian theory on the tendency of the propensity to save to increase as income increases. While valid for Type III it is not valid for Type V. The implication for the doctrine of the propensity to consume is discussed below in Chapter IV.

J. Behaviour of the Overall Incremental Capital-Output Ratio over Time under Different Patterns of Growth

The overall incremental capital-output ratio (ICOR) in any time t is always given by the formula

$$k_t = \frac{I_0\,(1+r_i)^t}{Y_0\,(1+r_y)^{t+1}-(1+r_y)^t}$$

$$\text{or} \quad k_t = \frac{I_0}{r_y Y_0} \left(\frac{1 + r_i}{1 + r_y}\right)^t$$

which reduces to,

$$k_t = k_0 \left(\frac{1 + r_i}{1 + r_y}\right)^t \tag{16}$$

$$\text{since} \quad \frac{I_0}{r_y Y_0} = k_0$$

Thus, given the capital coefficent, k_0, in time $t = 0$, we can derive the capital coefficient for the different patterns of growth for any subsequent period of time t as follows:

For Type III

$$k_t = k_0 \left(\frac{1 + r_i}{1 + r_y}\right)^t = k_0 \left\{\frac{1 + r_y(1 + \alpha C_0 / I_0)}{1 + r_y}\right\}^t$$

$$\text{i.e.,} \quad k_t = k_0 \left\{1 + \frac{\alpha r_y C_0 / I_0}{1 + r_y}\right\}^t \quad (16.1) \text{ (Type III)}$$

For Type IV

$$k_t = k_0 \tag{16.2} \text{ (Type IV)}$$

$$\text{since} \quad r_y = r_i = r_c$$

For Type V

$$k_t = k_0 \left(\frac{1 + r_i}{1 + r_y}\right)^t = k_0 \left\{\frac{1 + r_y(1 - \alpha)}{1 + r_y}\right\}^t$$

$$\text{i.e.,} \quad k_t = k_0 \left\{1 - \frac{\alpha r_y}{1 + r_y}\right\}^t$$

$$(16.3) \text{ (Type V)}$$

The respective rates of growth of k_t for the different patterns of growth are, accordingly,

$$r_{k_t} = \frac{\alpha r_y C_0 / I_0}{1 + r_y} \qquad \text{(Type III)}$$

$$r_{k_t} = 0 \qquad \text{(Type IV)}$$

and

$$r_{k_t} = \frac{-\alpha r_y}{1 + r_y} \qquad \text{(Type V)}$$

The savings ratio and the overall incremental capital-output ratio are thus seen to have the same rate of growth under each type of growth.

We may conclude, therefore, that the generally presumed constancy of the savings ratio (or investment coefficient) and the overall incremental capital-output ratio over time at given different rates of growth of aggregate output, consumption, and investment is not valid except under the conditions of steady growth. These coefficients must increase over time in a Type III economy and decrease over time in a Type V economy at given different rates of growth of aggregate output and its components. Consequently, also, the overall average capital-output ratio must follow the same pattern of behaviour corresponding to that of the incremental capital-output ratio in each type of economy. (Exception is made for the formally transformed Type V economy which behaves like a Type IV, with a constant aggregate and marginal ICOR).

K. Behaviour of the Keynesian Multiplier over
    Time under Different Patterns of Growth

By examining the rates of growth of Y and I one could tell at first glance how the investment multiplier would behave under the different patterns of growth.

One is therefore entitled to conclude that the value of the multiplier would decline over time in a Type III economy because $r_y < r_i$, remain constant under steady growth because $r_y = r_i$, and increase in a Type V economy because $r_y > r_i$. This conclusion can be verified for each of the growth types.

The general formula for the Keynesian investment multiplier in period t is given by

$$\left(\frac{\Delta Y}{\Delta I}\right)_t = \frac{Y_0}{I_0}\frac{\{(1+r_y)^t - (1+r_y)^{t-1}\}}{\{(1+r_i)^t - (1+r_i)^{t-1}\}}$$

$$\text{or} \quad \left(\frac{\Delta Y}{\Delta I}\right)_t = \frac{r_y Y_0 (1+r_y)^{t-1}}{r_i I_0 (1+r_i)^{t-1}} \tag{17}$$

According as we are dealing with Type III, IV, or V, r_y and r_i are respectively

$$r_y, \ r_y(1+\alpha C_0/I_0); \ r_y, \ r_y; \ \text{and} \ r_y, \ r_y(1-\alpha)$$

Under these conditions, and after suitable manipulations, equation 17 becomes

$$\left(\frac{\Delta Y}{\Delta I}\right)_t = \frac{r_y Y_0}{r_i I_0}\left\{1 - \frac{\alpha r_y C_0/I_0}{1 + r_i}\right\}^{t-1} \tag{17.1 (Type III)}$$

$$\text{or}\left(\frac{\Delta Y}{\Delta I}\right)_t = \frac{Y_0}{I_0} \tag{17.2 (Type IV)}$$

$$\text{or}\left(\frac{\Delta Y}{\Delta I}\right)_t = \frac{r_y Y_0}{r_y I_0}\left\{1 + \frac{\alpha r_y}{1 + r_i}\right\}^{t-1} \tag{17.3 (Type V)}$$

We therefore see that in a Type III economy the rate of growth of the investment multiplier is negative, zero in a Type IV economy (or a Type V formally transformed into a Type IV), and positive in a Type V economy. In short, the Keynesian multiplier must decrease over time in a Type III economy, remain constant in a Type IV, and increase in a Type V economy.13

L. Notes on Chapter III

(1) Magnitude of Technological Investment

Because of the conventional definition of investment as new productive equipment for civilian use and change in stocks in building construction which is adopted in the national accounts of many countries as well as in the United Nations System of National Accounts, and the associated convention of excluding capital expenditures on defence from investment, it is not easy to obtain an idea of the magnitude of the total investment actually made in scientific research and technological progress in countries adopting these procedures. Some part of such expenditures will take the form of wages paid to scientists and research workers and will be included with consumption expenditures. Another part will take

---

13. The implication here is that in a Type III economy successive doses of investment would peter out eventually because of the weak or declining effect of the multiplier in this type of economy. In this type of economy, therefore, the Keynesian argument against pump-priming (a once-for-all dose of investment) to revive aggregate demand where growth flags would be appropriate. In a Type V economy, however, the implication is in the opposite sense: the multiplier effect of each successive dose of investment gathers strength so that pump-priming would not sound out of place in such an economy; at least, it would require fewer doses of investment to revive a Type V than a Type III economy. However, as we shall subsequently see, if this is not already apparent, these points are academic from the point of view of the theory of continuous growth, which is our concern. For we are interested in specifying the conditions and mechanisms whereby growth becomes perpetual without any tendency to a weakening of its force.

the form of expenditure on research laboratories, equipment, and materials and will be treated partly as investment and partly as consumption expenditures on goods (materials). Yet another part, such as expenditures on military equipment related to research and development, may either be included in government consumption expenditures or excluded from the accounts for considerations of military strategy and concealed as "classified" information.

It is clear, therefore, that part of the information required is already massed with other data in the national accounts under investment or under consumption expenditures, but some of it is likely to be omitted. From the point of view of technological investment, all such expenditures, whether included in the national accounts or not, should properly be classified an investment, regardless of whether they take the form of consumption or investment in the narrow, conventional sense.

For the purpose of determining the magnitude of technological investment it would be necessary to classify under a separate category, or sub-category, of investment in the national accounts all expenditures on scientific research in the broad sense and on Research and Development in the limited conventional sense, whether spent on goods and services or on new equipment, and whether on military or civilian account. Only so will it become possible to fit this category of investment into the framework of the theory which has been elaborated in this and preceding chapters. An enormous job of sorting out the data would necessarily be involved, even with electronic computers, so far as expenditures for past years are concerned. But data for future years should be easily taken care of by appropriate provision on tax forms, business accounts, and other records.

In view of the fact that research expenditures may often take long to bear concrete results in the form of a usable, saleable product, and that a good deal of research is often of the basic kind which aims merely to extend the bounds of knowledge, without there being necessarily involved a desire for a concrete end-product, it may be difficult to identify the counterpart of such expenditures on the income side (value added) of the national accounts. The income aspect will only be notional for the most part, arrived at residually, in order to keep the two sides of the accounts in balance.

However, all the difficulties which may be encountered in an attempt to reconstruct past data can be avoided, as the general theory of growth patterns enables us to arrive at estimates of the proper depreciation and obsolescence coefficients and of the level of technological investment appropriate to the data. It is this advantage that endows it with an interest for planners and gives them, as well, broad guidelines for the future in their target-setting exercises for the economy as a whole. Within the broad target for technological investment they could proceed to formulate sectorial targets and thus on to targets for individual enterprises and projetcs. Thus the process of disaggregation would become complete and consistent with the overall target within the framework of the general theory of growth patterns. The relevance of all this to interindustry analysis hardly needs to be argued.

(2) Coefficient of Replacement, π

If K_t is the volume of capital stock in existence in the production period t, and π (a positive fraction) the proportion of the capital stock which is annually replaced as a result of depreciation and obsolescence, then the volume of capital stock in existence in the production period t is made up of the unconsumed and non-obsolete capital carried over from the preceding production period t-1, plus the aggregate investment in period t. In short,

$$K_t = (1-\pi)K_{t-1} + I_t$$

i.e. $I_t/r_y = (1-\pi)I_{t-1}/r_y + I_t$

or, $I_t/r_y = (1-\pi)I_t/r_y(1+r_i) + I_t$

or, $(1+r_i)=(1-\pi) + r_y(1+r_i)$

whence $\pi = r_i r_y + r_y - r_i$

The value of π will be positive or negative according as

$$r_i r_y + r_y - r_i \gtrless 0$$

In the former case, π is positive, provided

$$r_i r_y + r_y - r_i > 0$$

or, $r_y(1+r_i) > r_i$

or, $r_y > r_i/(1+r_i)$

which is always true when $r_y > r_i$ (Type V Growth).

In the latter case, π is negative, provided

$$r_i r_y + r_y - r_i < 0$$

or, $r_y < r_i(1-r_y)$

or, $r_y/(1-r_y) < r_i$

which is always true when $r_y < r_i$ (Type III Growth).

Regardless of the type of growth involved, π must always be a positive fractional quantity since replacement (depreciation plus obsolescence) is always a positive quantity. This condition is met only if $r_i = r_y$, and, consequently, $\pi = r_y^2$, a value which is always positive no matter what type of growth may be involved. The value $r_i = r_y$ is the case of Type IV, which is a limiting case of, and therefore common to, both Types III and V. It is therefore the value of r_i which is relevant to the calculation of the proportion of replacement in the total capital stock, regardless of whether the same economy grows on Type III or Type V.

The value $\pi = r_y^2$ has been used throughout our investigation of the investment model, although it was more simply derived by the elementary method of analogy.

(3) Recovery Period of Capital

In socialist countries the recovery period of capital is defined as the capital-output ratio. This, however, seems mistaken. For the recovery period of existing capital at any time t, namely K_t, is the time it would take to recover the value of this capital (at constant prices) at the current level and rate of growth of investment, that is, at the level I_t growing at the annual rate of r_i. This definition of the capital recovery period follows naturally from the fact that K_t produces an income, Y_t of which C_t is consumed, leaving I_t as the current addition to the capital stock. It is at this current rate of addition to the capital stock growing at the rate r_i that the existing volume of capital, K_t, will be recovered in n years.

Thus the capital recovery factor is given by the capital-investment ratio, K_t/I_t, and not by the capital-output ratio, K_t/Y_t. Accordingly,

$$K_t = I_t + I_t(1+r_i) + I_t(1+r_i)^2 + \ldots + I_t(1+r_i)^{n-1}$$

$$= I_t\left[1 + (1+r_i) + (1+r_i)^2 + \ldots + (1+r_i)^{n-1}\right]$$

$$(1+r_i) K_t = I_t\left[(1+r_i) + (1+r_i)^2 + (1+r_i)^3 + \ldots + (1+r_i)^n\right]$$

Substracting the first series from the second, we have

$$r_i K_t = I_t\left[(1+r_i)^n - 1\right]$$

But $K_t/I_t = 1/r_y$

Hence $r_i/r_y = (1+r_i)^n - 1$

or $(1+r_i)^n = (r_i+r_y)/r_y$

whence $$n = \frac{\log(r_i+r_y) - \log r_y}{\log(1+r_i)}$$

If incremental technological investment is included in aggregate investment, then investment grows at the rate of r_i in Type III and r_y in Type V. Hence the formula just derived holds for Type III, and for Type V when we substitute $r_i = r_y$. In the latter case, the formula becomes:

$$n = \frac{\log 2r_y - \log r_y}{\log (1+r_y)}$$

or $n = \log 2/\log (1+r_y)$

We therefore arrive at the following formulae for the recovery period of capital for the two main types of growth:

Type III: $n = \dfrac{\log (r_i+r_y) - \log r_y}{\log (1+r_i)}$

Type V: $n = \log 2/ \log (1+r_y)$

(4) Recovery Period of Investment

The aggregate investment at any time t is I_t. This increases at the annual rate of r_i, so that the incremental growth is $r_i I_t$. The rate of recovery of I_t is therefore $r_i I_t$ which itself grows at the rate of r_i.

Hence, using the sinking fund formula as in the preceding cases

$$r_i I_t = \frac{r_i}{(1+r_i)^{n-1}} I_t$$

or $(1+r_i)^n = 2$

whence $n = \log 2/\log (1+r_i)$

With incremental technological investment included in aggregate investment, I_t grows at the rate of r_i in Type III but at the rate of r_y in Type V. Hence the formula just derived holds for Type III, and for Type V if we substitute $r_i = r_y$. In the latter case the formula becomes

$$n = \log 2 / \log (1+r_y)$$

The formulae for the recovery period of investment for the two main patterns of growth are therefore the following:

$$\text{Type III: } n = \log 2 / \log (1+r_i)$$

$$\text{Type V: } n = \log 2 / \log (1+r_y)$$

Comparing these formulae with the corresponding formulae for the recovery period of capital for the two types of growth given in (3) preceding, we have :

Recovery Period of Capital	*Recovery Period of Investment*
Type III $\quad n = \dfrac{\log (r_i + r_y) - \log r_y}{\log (1+r_i)}$	$n = \log 2 / \log(1+r_i)$
Type V $\quad n = \log 2 / \log (1+r_y)$	$n = \log 2 / \log(1+r_y)$

We therefore see that the recovery period is the same for capital and for investment in Type V but not in Type III where the period is slightly longer for capital than for investment. Nevertheless, the formula for the recovery period of investment is also a good approximation for the recovery period of capital in Type III, provided $r_i - r_y \lessgtr 0.05 r_y$.

IV
CONSUMPTION PROGRAMME FOR THE DIFFERENT PATTERNS OF GROWTH

A.   Deriving the Consumption Programme

We have seen that the rates of growth of consumption vary according to the pattern of growth of an economy, as follows:

$$\text{Type III} : r_c = r_y(1-\alpha)$$
$$\text{Type IV} : r_c = r_y$$
$$\text{Type V} : r_c = r_y(1+\alpha I_0/C_0)$$

With this information we may proceed to formulate the consumption requirements for the different growth patterns.

Type III

For this type of economy the consumption formula is given by

$$C_t = \left\{ 1+r_y(1-\alpha) \right\}^t C_0 \qquad (18)$$

Writing t = 1, we obtain :

$$C_1 = \left\{ 1+r_y(1-\alpha) \right\} C_0$$
$$\text{or}$$
$$C_1 = C_0 + r_y C_0 - \alpha r_y C_0 \qquad (19)$$

which indicates that in the conditions of Type III growth, aggregate Consumption in period 1 (or any period for that matter) is *less* than the sum of aggregate consumption in the preceding period and the increment therein at the rate of r_y by the provision for incremental technological investment in the current period. Which is only to be expected if the income equation of the current period is to remain in balance, that is,

$$Y_1 = Y_0 + r_y Y_0 = \left\{ C_0 + r_y C_0 - \alpha r_y C_0 \right\} + \left\{ I_0 + r_y I_0 + \alpha r_y C_0 \right\}$$
$$= (1+r_y)C_0 + (1+r_y)I_0.$$

The quantity $\alpha r_y C_0$ is, of course, equal to $(1-\mu)r_y I_0$, the incremental technological investment, since $\alpha = (1-\mu)I_0/C_0$.

It has been demonstrated in the preceding chapter that for a continuation of the Type III pattern r_c cannot fall as low as r_y $(1-I_0/C_0)$, and that r_p cannot exceed this same value if per capita consumption is to increase continually, as well as per capita income and investment.

Type IV   .

We do not need to examine this case in detail. As a limiting case of growth in which $r_c = r_y = r_i$, it may be interpreted as a case where *either* there is no incremental growth in technological investment or such investment is indeterminate. Nor is it possible to specify precisely the limit of the population growth rate which should permit a continuing growth in the real standard of living (see Chapter IV).

Type V

The consumption programme for Type V is given by

$$C_t = \left\{1 + r_y(1 + \alpha I_0/C_0)\right\}^t C_0 \qquad (20)$$

Writing $t=1$, we obtain

$$C_1 = \left\{1 + r_y(1 + \alpha I_0/C_0)\right\} C_0$$
or $\qquad\qquad\qquad\qquad\qquad\qquad\qquad (21)$
$$C_1 = C_0 + r_y C_0 + \alpha r_y I_0$$

Equation 21 indicates that aggregate consumption in period 1 (or any period) is compounded of aggregate consumption in the preceding period, the increment therein at the rate of r_y, and an allowance for incremental technological investment. The adjustment for incremental technological investment is made by an equivalent reduction in the aggregate investment of the current period, thus leaving the latter just adequate to cover the current period's net investment and replacement. In the process of adjustment the balance of the income equation is maintained, so that

$$Y_1 = Y_0 + r_y Y_0 = \{C_0 + r_y C_0 + \alpha r_y I_0\} + \{I_0 + r_y I_0 - \alpha r_y I_0\}$$

$$= (1+r_y)C_0 + (1+r_y)I_0$$

The quantity $\alpha r_y I_0$ is equal to $\left(\frac{1-\mu}{2}\right) r_y I_0$, or to $(\mu-1)r_y I_0$, according as $1 > \mu > 0$, or $2 > \mu > 1$.

If any general conclusion is possible on the basis of the consumption requirements for Type III and for Type V, it is that a Type III economy is likely to accentuate a policy of planned obsolescence of investment, subsidized out of consumption, while a Type V economy is likely to accentuate a policy of planned obsolescence of consumption, subsidized out of investment. This is the logical conclusion which our investigation leads to, assuming that technological investment does figure importantly in the growth process of an economy of one type or the other. Further studies will need to be made to test this conclusion, but one may at first glance seem to observe some semblance of support in the case of, say, the United Kingdom (Type III) or the United States (Type V) while these economies continue in their respective patterns.

B. Behaviour of the Propensity to Consume over
    Time under Different Patterns of Growth

The growth of consumption over time involves certain implications for the behaviour of the overall marginal propensity to consume which, at any period t, is given by the following:

$$\left(\frac{\Delta C}{\Delta Y}\right)_t = \frac{C_0 \left\{(1+r_0)^t - (1+r_0)^{t-1}\right\}}{Y_0 \left\{(1+r_y)^t - (1+r_y)^{t-1}\right\}}$$

or

$$\left(\frac{\Delta C}{\Delta Y}\right)_t = \frac{r_c}{r_y}\left(\frac{1+r_c}{1+r_y}\right)^{t-1}\frac{C_0}{Y_0} \tag{22}$$

According as we are dealing with Type III, Type IV, or Type V growth, the growth rate of consumption is, respectively, equal to

$$r_y(1-\alpha), \ r_y, \ \text{or} \ r_y(1+\alpha I_0/C_0)$$

Under these conditions, Equation 22 becomes

$$\left(\frac{\Delta C}{\Delta Y}\right)_t = (1-\alpha)\left(1-\frac{\alpha r_y}{1+r_y}\right)^{t-1}\frac{C_0}{Y_0} \qquad \begin{matrix}(22.1)\\ (\text{Type III})\end{matrix}$$

or

$$\left(\frac{\Delta C}{\Delta Y}\right)_t = \frac{C_0}{Y_0} \qquad \begin{matrix}(22.2)\\ (\text{Type IV})\end{matrix}$$

or

$$\left(\frac{\Delta C}{\Delta Y}\right)_t = (1+\alpha I_0/C_0)\left(1+\frac{\alpha r_y I_0/C_0}{1+r_y}\right)^{t-1}\frac{C_0}{Y_0} \qquad \begin{matrix}(22.3)\\ (\text{Type}\\ \text{V})\end{matrix}$$

It is clear, therefore, that in a Type III economy the marginal propensity to consume will fall over time because its rate of growth is negative. This implies, also, that the average propensity to consume will likewise decline over time in Type III.

In Type IV the marginal and average propensities to consume will remain constant at C_0/Y_0, since the rate of growth of the marginal propensity to consume is zero.

In Type V, however, the growth rate of the marginal propensity to consume is positive. Hence both marginal and average propensities to consume will increase over time in a Type V economy.

The same conclusions regarding the trend of change in marginal and in average propensity to consume can be arrived at *prima facie,* on the ground that the growth rate of consumption is less than the growth rate of output in Type III, and greater in Type V.

The decline of the marginal propensity to consume over time in a Type III economy may well be due to the increasing deductions to be made from aggregate consumption for investment in technology. For the opposite reason, the marginal propensity to consume must increase over time in a Type V economy because of the increasing impact of obsolescence on consumption goods which must be made up out of deductions from aggregate investment destined to augment technological investment.

In order to complete the discussion it is necessary to state the formulae for the average propensity to consume for the different growth patterns. In general the formula is given by

$$\left(\frac{C}{Y}\right)_t = \frac{C_0}{Y_0}\left(\frac{1+r_c}{1+r_y}\right)^t \tag{23}$$

which becomes

$$\left(\frac{C}{Y}\right)_t = \frac{C_0}{Y_0}\left(1-\frac{\alpha r_y}{1+r_y}\right)^t \qquad \text{(23.1) (Type III)}$$

or

$$\left(\frac{C}{Y}\right)_t = \frac{C_0}{Y_0} \qquad \text{(23.2) (Type IV)}$$

or

$$\left(\frac{C}{Y}\right)_t = \frac{C_0}{Y_0}\left(1 + \frac{\alpha r_y I_0/C_0}{1 + r_y}\right)^t \quad (23.3) \text{ (Type V)}$$

Our results are of great interest because they throw considerable light on the Keynesian doctrine of the propensity to consume. Keynes's dictum about the falling marginal propensity to consume as a society becomes richer (in other words, as growth proceeds) [1] is seen to be valid only for a Type III economy but not for a Type V. It may thus hold true for the United Kingdom and the six countries of the European Economic Community according to the evidence in Table I (while these countries continue in the Type III pattern of growth) but not for Type V economies like those of the Federal Republic of Germany, Canada, and the United States (again, while these countries continue in that pattern). It would similarly hold for developing countries in a Type III growth pattern but not for those in a Type V (see Table II).

Doubt is also cast on the presumed psychological basis of the dictum as claimed by Keynes. It turns out, after all, that there is nothing psychological about the behaviour pattern of the marginal propensity to consume.

Our results also raise basic issues regarding the role of taxation in income redistribution, especially the justification on the basis of Keynesian theory of progressive taxation of incomes in order to achieve a transfer from higher to lower income groups, on the basis of an assumed inverse correlation between size of income and the marginal propensity to consume. Progressive income taxation, on the basis of a falling marginal propensity to consume, and its attendant distributive policies, can no longer be assumed valid for all types of economies. It may be valid for a Type III but not for a Type V economy. Even if one regarded a

1. J.M. Keynes, *The General Theory of Employment, Interest and Money*, Harcourt, Brace & Co., pp. 27, 31, 96.

Type V as being formally transformable into a Type IV, one ends up with a constant marginal (and, therefore, average) propensity to consume, instead of an increasing or decreasing marginal propensity to consume; and this would seem to support a regime of proportional taxation according to the classical doctrine enunciated by Adam Smith, the result of which would be to leave the distribution of income unaltered.

Furthermore, if the trend towards an increasing marginal propensity to consume in a Type V economy is accepted, this could be regarded by some as constituting an argument for regressive taxation of incomes in this type of economy, assuming that what is true for the economy as a whole over time is also true of the income of individuals as growth proceeds. But whether or not this assumption is valid, the case for progressive taxation of incomes in a Type V economy, once its justification (or, rather the lack of it) is demonstrated on the basis of the trend of the marginal propensity to comsume over time, will have to be made on other grounds; for example, on the basis of its much greater efficiency, from a revenue point of view, than any other alternative system of taxation. [2] In particular, and from consideration of the long-term trend of the marginal propensity to consume, a case may be made, at least, for a proportional income tax (which leaves the distribution of income unaltered) in those economies, both developed and developing, which proceed on a Type V growth pattern - so long as they continue within this pattern.

C.   Behaviour of the Conventional Accelerator over
      Time in the Different Patterns of Growth

Prima facie, since the accelerator involves the ratio of ΔI to ΔC, we may arrive at the conclusion that

---

2. This point as well as the general basis and types of income taxation has been fully discussed in my paper entitled, "Marginal Utility, Interpersonal Comparisons and the Theory of Taxation", *The American Journal of Economics and Sociology,* Vol. 22, No. 1, January 1963, pp. 173-183.

in a Type III economy the accelerator must increase over time, because the rate of growth of investment exceeds that of consumption; remain constant in Type IV, investment and consumption growing at the same rate; and decline in Type V where investment grows at a rate less than that of consumption. These conclusions are demonstrated as follows.

The general formula for the accelerator[3] in period t is given by

$$\left(\frac{\Delta I}{\Delta C_t} \right) = \frac{I_0}{C_0} \left\{ \frac{(1+r_i)^t - (1+r_i)^{t-1}}{(1+r_c)^t - (1+r_c)^{t-1}} \right\}$$

or

$$\left(\frac{\Delta I}{\Delta C} \right)_t = \frac{r_i}{r_c} \left(\frac{1+r_i}{1+r_c} \right)^{t-1} \frac{I_0}{C_0} \qquad (24)$$

With appropriate manipulations this becomes

$$\left(\frac{\Delta I}{\Delta C} \right)_t = \frac{r_i}{r_c} \left(1 + \frac{\alpha r_y Y_0/I_0}{1 + r_c} \right)^{t-1} \frac{I_0}{C_0} \qquad \begin{array}{l} (24.1) \\ \text{(Type III)} \end{array}$$

or

$$\left(\frac{\Delta I}{\Delta C} \right)_t = \frac{I_0}{C_0} \qquad \begin{array}{l} (24.2) \\ \text{(Type IV)} \end{array}$$

---

[3] As conventionally measured

or

$$\left(\frac{\Delta I}{\Delta C}\right)_t = \frac{r_i}{r_c}\left(1 - \frac{\alpha\, r_y Y_0 / C_0}{1 + r_c}\right)^{t-1}\frac{I_0}{C_0} \qquad \begin{array}{c}(24.3)\\ (\text{Type V})\end{array}$$

Thus, in Type III the accelerator will increase with time, its rate of growth being positive, remain constant in Type IV, and decrease with time in Type V where its rate of growth is negative.

D.   Interaction of the Multiplier and the Accelerator
     Over Time in the Different Patterns of Growth

In considering the interaction of the multiplier and the accelerator, we find an increasing accelerator matched by a decreasing multiplier in a Type III economy, and a decreasing accelerator matched by an increasing multiplier in a Type V economy. These opposing tendencies balance out in a net interaction, $\Delta Y/\Delta C$. We are therefore entitled to conclude that in a Type III economy the net effect of the interaction of the multiplier and the accelerator is likely to be greater than in a Type V economy. This is because the rate of growth of consumption is relatively less than that of aggregate output in Type III, but relatively greater in Type V. In the former type the interaction effect will increase over time and decline in the latter type. These conclusions are demonstrated below.

The interaction of the multiplier and the accelerator, $\frac{\Delta Y}{\Delta I} \cdot \frac{\Delta I}{\Delta C}$, i.e., $\frac{\Delta Y}{\Delta C}$, over time is given by the formula

$$\left(\frac{\Delta Y}{\Delta C}\right)_t = \frac{Y_0}{C_0}\left\{\frac{(1+r_y)^t - (1+r_y)^{t-1}}{(1+r_c)^t - (1+r_y)^{t-1}}\right\}$$

or

$$\left(\frac{\Delta Y}{\Delta C}\right)_t = \frac{r_y}{r_c}\left(\frac{1+r_y}{1+r_c}\right)^{t-1}\frac{Y_0}{C_0} \tag{25}$$

This becomes, after appropriate manipulations,

$$\left(\frac{\Delta Y}{\Delta C}\right)_t = \frac{r_y}{r_c}\left(1+\frac{\alpha r_y}{1+r_c}\right)^{t-1}\frac{Y_0}{C_0} \qquad \begin{array}{l}(25.1)\\ \text{(Type III)}\end{array}$$

or

$$\left(\frac{\Delta Y}{\Delta C}\right)_t = \frac{Y_0}{C_0} \qquad \begin{array}{l}(25.2)\\ \text{(Type IV)}\end{array}$$

or

$$\left(\frac{\Delta Y}{\Delta C}\right)_t = \frac{r_y}{r_c}\, 1-\left(\frac{\alpha r_y I_0/C_0}{1+r_c}\right)^{t-1}\frac{Y_0}{C_0} \qquad \begin{array}{l}(25.3)\\ \text{(Type V)}\end{array}$$

V
SUMMARY OF RESULTS

The main results and conclusions of the discussion in Part One can now be conveniently summarized in a schedule for the two main types of growth. The schedule serves as a ready reference of appropriate formulae for use in computing the values of the various quantities and coefficients.

Quantities and Coefficients	Type III		Type V	
	$r_i > r_y > r_c$ $\qquad$ $1 > \mu > 0$ $\qquad$ $1 > \alpha > 0$	$1 > \mu > 0$ $\qquad$ $1 > \alpha > 0$	$r_c > r_y > r_i$ $\qquad$ $1 > \alpha > 0$	$2 > \mu > 1$
Base year Y, C, and I	Y_o, C_o, and I_o		Y_o, C_o, and I_o	
Rate of Growth of Y	$r_y = r_p + r_w$		$r_y = r_p + r_w$	
Rate of Growth of C	$r_c = r_y(1-\alpha)$	$r_y(1+0.5I_o/C_o) > r_c > r_y$	$r_c = r_y(1+\alpha I_o/C_o)$	$r_y(1+I_o/C_o) > r_c > r_y$
Rate of Growth of I	$r_i = r_y(1+\alpha C_o/I_o)$	$r_y > r_i > 0.5r_y$	$r_i = r_y(1-\alpha)$	$r_y > r_i > r_y(1-I_o/C_o)$
α	$I_o/C_o > \alpha = \dfrac{r_i-r_c}{r_y}\cdot\dfrac{I_o}{Y_o} > 0$ $\dfrac{Y_o}{r_i-r_c} = \dfrac{C_o}{r_i-r_c-\alpha r_y} = \dfrac{I_o}{\alpha r_y} > 0$	$0.5r_y > \alpha > 0$	$\alpha = \dfrac{r_c-r_i}{r_y}\cdot\dfrac{C_o}{Y_o}$ $\dfrac{Y_o}{r_c-r_i} = \dfrac{C_o}{\alpha r_y} = \dfrac{I_o}{r_c-r_i-\alpha r_y}$	$1 > \alpha > 0$
Coefficient of Depreciation = μ	$\mu = 1-\alpha C_o/I_o = \dfrac{r_y(1+\alpha)-r_i+r_c}{r_y}$	$\mu = 1 - 2\alpha$	$\mu = 1 + \alpha$	
Coefficient of Obsolescence Coefficient of Technological Invest. } λ	$\lambda = 1-\mu = \alpha C_o/I_o = \dfrac{r_i-r_c-\alpha r_y}{r_y}$	$\lambda = \alpha = (1-\mu)/2$	$\lambda = \alpha = \mu - 1$	
Base year Population (P)	P_o		P_o	
Rate of Growth of P	r_p		r_p	

Maximum Rate of Growth of P	$r_p(max) = r_y(1-I_o/C_o) = r_y\left(\dfrac{r_i-r_c-2\alpha r_y}{r_i-r_c-\alpha r_y}\right)$	$r_p(max) = 0.5r_y$ $r_p(max) = r_y(1-I_o/C_o)$ $= (r_i-r_c-2\alpha r_y)/\alpha$
*Minimum Rate of Growth of Net Y	$r_w(min) = r_y - r_p = r_y I_o/C_o = r_{yo}I_o/I_o = \dfrac{\alpha r_y^2}{r_i-r_c-\alpha r_y}$	$r_w(min) = r_y - r_p = 0.5r_y$ $= (r_c-r_i-\alpha r_y)/\alpha$
Coefficient of Replacement	$\mu + \lambda = \mu + \alpha C_o/I_o = 1$	$\mu + \lambda = 1-\alpha$ $\mu + \lambda = 1+2\alpha$
Coefficient of Replacement & Tech. Investment	$\mu + 2\lambda = 2-\mu = 1+\alpha C_o/I_o = \dfrac{r_y(1-\alpha)+r_i-r_c}{r_y}$	$\mu + 2\lambda = 1$ $\mu + 2\lambda = 1+3\alpha$
Depreciation = D_t	$\mu r_y I_{t-1} = \mu r_{yo} I_o (1+r_i)^{t-1}$	$\mu r_y I_{t-1} = \mu r_{yo} I_o (1+r_i)^{t-1}$
Obsolescence Marginal Tech. Invest. $\Big\} o_t^r = (\Delta T)_t$	$\alpha r_y \dfrac{C_o}{I_o} I_{t-1}$	$\alpha r_y I_{t-1}$
Replacement = R_t	$r_y I_{t-1}$	$(1-\alpha)r_y I_{t-1} = r_i I_{t-1}$ $(1+2\alpha)r_y I_{t-1}$
Net Investment = N_t	$I_{t-1} = I_o(1+r_i)^{t-1}$	$I_{t-1} = I_o(1+r_i)^{t-1}$
Gross Investment (incl. ΔT) = i_t	$\Big\{ I_t = I_o(1+r_i)^t$	$(1+r_y)I_{t-1} = I_o(1+r_y)(1+r_i)^{t-1}$
Gross Invest. (incl. ΔT as from $\bar{t}=0$) = $\hat{i}_t$	$\Big\} \hat{i}_t = I_o(1+r_i)^t$	$i_o(1+r_y)^t = I_o(1+r_y)^{t+1}/(1+r_i)^t$

Quantities and Coefficients	Type III	Type V
Gross Invest. (excl. ΔT) = I_t	$I_t = (1+r_y)\,I_{t-1} = I_o(1+r_i)(1+r_i)^{t-1}$	$I = I_t = I_o(1+r_i)^t$; $\dot{I}_t$
Consumption (incl. ΔT) = $\dot{C}_t$	$\dot{C}_t = (1+r_y)\,C_{t-1} = C_o(1+r_y)(1+r_c)^{t-1}$	$\dot{C}_t = C_t = C_o(1+r_c)^t$
Consumption (excl. ΔT) = C_t	$\Big\{\; C_t = C_o(1+r_c)^t$	$C_t = (1+r_y)\,C_{t-1} = C_o(1+r_y)(1+r_c)^{t-1}$
Consumption (excl. ΔT) as from t=0) = $\check{C}_t$	$\check{C}_t = C_t = C_o(1+r_c)^t$	$\check{C}_t = C_o(1+r_y)^t = C_o(1+r_y)^{t+1}/(1+r_c)$
Contribution of Tech. Investment to Y	$\alpha\, r_y\, C_o / r_i I_o$	α
Aggregate Technological Investment = T_t	$T_t = \dfrac{1+r_i}{r_i}(\Delta T)_t = \dfrac{\alpha r_y C_o}{r_i I_o} I_t$	$T_t = \dfrac{1+r_y}{r_y}(\Delta T)_t = \alpha\,\dot{I}_t = \alpha(1+r_y)(1+r_i)^{t-1} I_o$
Aggregate non-Tech. Invest. = $I_t - T_t$	$\left(1 - \dfrac{\alpha r_y C_o}{r_i I_o}\right) I_t = \dfrac{r_y}{r_i}\, I_t$	$(1-\alpha)\,\dot{I}_t = (1-\alpha)(1+r_y)(1+r_i)^{t-1} I_o$
Value of Capital Stock = K_t	$K_t = I_t / r_y = I_o(1+r_i)^t / r_y$	$K_t = \dot{I}_t / r_y = \dot{I}_o(1+r_y)^t / r_y = I_o(1+r_y)^{t+1}/r_y(1+r_i)^t$
Overall ICOR = $\left(\dfrac{I}{\Delta Y}\right)_t = k_t$	$k_t = k_o\left(\dfrac{1+r_i}{1+r_y}\right)^t = k_o\left(1 + \dfrac{\alpha r_y C_o / I_o}{1+r_y}\right)^t$ $\left[\text{where } k_o = I_o / r_y Y_o\right]$	$k_t = k_o\left(\dfrac{1+r_i}{1+r_y}\right)^t = k_o\left(1 - \dfrac{\alpha r_y}{1+r_y}\right)^t$ $\left[\text{where } k_o = I_o / r_y Y_o\right]$
Aggregate Income = Y_t	$Y_t = Y_o(1+r_y)^t$	$Y_t = Y_o(1+r_y)^t$

$$\left(\frac{\Delta C}{\Delta Y}\right)_t = \frac{\Delta C_{t-1}}{\Delta Y_{t-1}} = \frac{r_c}{r_y}\left(\frac{1+r_c}{1+r_y}\right)^{t-1}\frac{C_0}{Y_0}$$

$$= (1+\alpha I_0/C_0)\left(1+\frac{\alpha r_y I_0/C_0}{1+r_y}\right)^{t-1}\frac{C_0}{Y_0}$$

$$\left(\frac{C}{Y}\right)_t = \frac{C_t}{Y_t} = \left(\frac{1+r_c}{1+r_y}\right)^t\frac{C_0}{Y_0} = \left(1+\frac{\alpha r_y I_0/C_0}{1+r_y}\right)^t\frac{C_0}{Y_0}$$

$$\left(\frac{\Delta S}{\Delta Y}\right)_t = 1-\frac{\Delta C_{t-1}}{\Delta Y_{t-1}} = \frac{r_i}{r_y}\left(\frac{1+r_i}{1+r_y}\right)^{t-1}\frac{I_0}{Y_0}$$

$$= (1-\alpha)\left(1-\frac{\alpha r_y}{1+r_y}\right)^{t-1}\frac{I_0}{Y_0}$$

$$\left(\frac{S}{Y}\right)_t = 1-\frac{C_t}{Y_t} = \left(\frac{1+r_i}{1+r_y}\right)^t\frac{I_0}{Y_0} = \left(1-\frac{\alpha r_y}{1+r_y}\right)^t\frac{I_0}{Y_0}$$

$$\left(\frac{\Delta C}{\Delta Y}\right)_t = \frac{\Delta C_{t-1}}{\Delta Y_{t-1}} = \frac{r_c}{r_y}\left(\frac{1+r_c}{1+r_y}\right)^{t-1}\frac{C_0}{Y_0}$$

$$= (1-\alpha)\left(1-\frac{\alpha r_y}{1+r_y}\right)^{t-1}\frac{C_0}{Y_0}$$

$$\left(\frac{C}{Y}\right)_t = \frac{C_t}{Y_t} = \left(\frac{1+r_c}{1+r_y}\right)^t\frac{C_0}{Y_0} = \left(1-\frac{\alpha r_y}{1+r_y}\right)^t\frac{C_0}{Y_0}$$

$$\left(\frac{\Delta S}{\Delta Y}\right)_t = 1-\frac{\Delta C_{t-1}}{\Delta Y_{t-1}} = \frac{r_i}{r_y}\left(\frac{1+r_i}{1+r_y}\right)^{t-1}\frac{I_0}{Y_0}$$

$$= (1+\alpha C_0/I_0)\left(1+\frac{\alpha r_y C_0/I_0}{1+r_y}\right)^{t-1}\frac{I_0}{Y_0}$$

$$\left(\frac{S}{Y}\right)_t = 1-\frac{C_t}{Y_t} = \left(\frac{1+r_i}{1+r_y}\right)^t\frac{I_0}{Y_0} = \left(1+\frac{\alpha r_y C_0/I_0}{1+r_y}\right)^t\frac{I_0}{Y_0}$$

$$\text{MPC} = \left(\frac{\Delta C}{\Delta Y}\right)_t$$

$$\text{APC} = \left(\frac{C}{Y}\right)_t$$

$$\text{MPS} = \text{MPI} = \left(\frac{\Delta S}{\Delta Y}\right)_t = \left(\frac{\Delta I}{\Delta Y}\right)_t$$

$$\text{APS} = \text{API} = \left(\frac{S}{Y}\right)_t = \left(\frac{I}{Y}\right)_t$$

Quantities and Coefficients	Type III	Type V
Investment Multiplier $=\left(\dfrac{\Delta Y}{\Delta I}\right)_t$	$\left(\dfrac{\Delta Y}{\Delta I}\right)_t = \dfrac{\Delta Y_{t-1}}{\Delta I_{t-1}} = \dfrac{r_y}{r_i}\left(\dfrac{1+r_y}{1+r_i}\right)^{t-1}\dfrac{Y_o}{I_o}$ $= \dfrac{r_y}{r_i}\left(1-\dfrac{\alpha r_y C/I_o}{1+r_i}\right)^{t-1}$	$\left(\dfrac{\Delta Y}{\Delta I}\right)_t = \dfrac{\Delta Y_{t-1}}{\Delta I_{t-1}} = \dfrac{r_y}{r_i}\left(\dfrac{1+r_y}{1+r_i}\right)^{t-1}\dfrac{Y_o}{I_o} = \dfrac{r_y}{r_i}\left(\dfrac{\alpha r_y}{1+r_i}\right)^{t-1}\dfrac{Y_o}{I_o}$
Accelerator $=\left(\dfrac{\Delta I}{\Delta C}\right)_t$	$\left(\dfrac{\Delta I}{\Delta C}\right)_t = \dfrac{\Delta I_{t-1}}{\Delta C_{t-1}} = \dfrac{r_i}{r_c}\left(\dfrac{1+r_i}{1+r_c}\right)^{t-1}\dfrac{I_o}{C_o}$ $= \dfrac{r_i}{r_c}\left(\dfrac{\alpha r_y C/I_o}{1+r_i}\right)^{t-1}$	$\left(\dfrac{\Delta I}{\Delta C}\right)_t = \dfrac{\Delta I_{t-1}}{\Delta C_{t-1}} = \dfrac{r_i}{r_c}\left(\dfrac{1+r_i}{1+r_c}\right)^{t-1}\dfrac{I_o}{C_o} = \dfrac{r_i}{r_c}\left(1-\dfrac{\alpha r_y Y_o/C_o}{1+r_c}\right)^{t-1}\dfrac{I_o}{C_o}$
Multiplier-cum-Accelerator $=\left(\dfrac{\Delta Y}{\Delta C}\right)_t$	$\left(\dfrac{\Delta Y}{\Delta C}\right)_t = \dfrac{\Delta Y_{t-1}}{\Delta C_{t-1}} = \dfrac{r_y}{r_c}\left(\dfrac{1+r_y}{1+r_c}\right)^{t-1}\dfrac{Y_o}{C_o}$ $= \dfrac{r_y}{r_c}\left(\dfrac{\alpha r_y}{1+r_c}\right)^{t-1}\dfrac{Y_o}{C_o}$	$\left(\dfrac{\Delta Y}{\Delta C}\right)_t = \dfrac{\Delta Y_{t-1}}{\Delta C_{t-1}} = \dfrac{r_y}{r_c}\left(\dfrac{1+r_y}{1+r_c}\right)^{t-1}\dfrac{Y_o}{C_o} = \dfrac{r_y}{r_c}\left(1-\dfrac{\alpha r_y Y_o/C_o}{1+r_c}\right)^{t-1}\dfrac{Y_o}{C_o}$
Rate of Growth of Gross $Y/P = r_{(Y/P)}$	$r_{(Y/P)} = \dfrac{r_y - r_p}{1+r_p} = \dfrac{r_y I_o/C_o}{1+r_y(1-I_o/C_o)}$	$r_{(Y/P)} = \dfrac{r_y - r_p}{1+r_p} = \dfrac{0.5\,r_y}{1+0.5 r_y}$ $r_{(Y/P)} = \dfrac{r_y - r_p}{1+r_p} = \dfrac{r_y I_o/C_o}{1+r_y(1-I_o/C_o)}$
*Rate of Growth of Net $Y = r_{(Y)\text{ net}}$	$r_{(Y)\text{ net}} = r_y - r_p = r_y I_o/C_o = r_w$	$r_{(Y)\text{ net}} = r_y - r_p = 0.5 r_y = r_w$ $r_{(y)\text{ net}} = r_y - r_p = r_y I_o/C_o = r_w$

Rate of Growth of Gross C/P = $r_{(C/P)}$	$r_{(C/P)} = \dfrac{r_c - r_p}{1+r_p} = \dfrac{r_y\,(I_o/C_o - \alpha)}{1+ r_y(1-I_o/C_o)}$	$r_{(C/P)} = \dfrac{r_c - r_p}{1+r_p} = \dfrac{r_y\,(0.5 + \alpha I_o/C_o)}{1+ 0.5\, r_y}$	$r_{(C/P)} = \dfrac{r_c - r_p}{1+r_p} = \dfrac{(1+\alpha)\,r_y\,I_o/C_o}{1+ r_y(1-I_o/C_o)}$
Rate of Growth of Net C = $r_{(C)net}$	$r_{(C)net} = r_c - r_p = r_y\,(I_o/C_o - \alpha)$	$r_{(C)net} = r_c - r_p = r_y(0.5 + \alpha I_o/C_o)$	$r_{(C)net} = r_c - r_p = (1+\alpha)\,r_y\,I_o/C_o$
Rate of Growth of Gross I/P = $r_{(I/P)}$	$r_{(I/P)} = \dfrac{r_i - r_p}{1+r_p} = \dfrac{r_y\,(\alpha C_o/I_o + I_o/C_o)}{1+ r_y(1-I_o/C_o)}$	$r_{(I/P)} = \dfrac{r_i - r_p}{1+r_p} = \dfrac{r_y\,(0.5 - \alpha)}{1+0.5\, r_y}$	$r_{(I/P)} = \dfrac{r_i - r_p}{1+r_p} = \dfrac{r_y\,(I_o/C_o - \alpha)}{1+ r_y(1-I_o/C_o)}$
Rate of Growth of Net I = $r_{(I)net}$	$r_{(I)net} = r_i - r_p = r_y\,(\alpha C_o/I_o + I_o/C_o)$	$r_{(I)net} = r_i - r_p = r_y\,(0.5 - \alpha)$	$r_{(I)net} = r_i - r_p = r_y\,(I_o/C_o - \alpha)$

*Identical

PART TWO

COMPARATIVE DYNAMICS OF GROWTH

VI

LONG-TERM AND SHORT-TERM CHANGES IN THE COEFFICIENTS OF GROWTH

So far our discussion in Part One has been limited to an investigation of the statics of growth. In other words, we have assumed given rates of growth of aggregate ouput, consumption, and investment. These rates once given are assumed to continue indefinitely into the future. That is to say, they are held constant over time. This confining assumption must now be relaxed in order to bring our theory closer to reality.

We shall now assume that the rate of growth of aggregate output r_y is subject to change—an increase or a decrease. Once r_y is thus allowed to vary, r_i and r_c must also vary, since r_y is a resultant of these rates which are also expressible in terms of r_y. Our principal interest is to determine what happens to the economy under the two main types of growth. In this investigation our knowledge of the inversion characteristics of these types should be of great help.

In this part of our study we are inevitably led to consider the oscillatory behaviour of the growth equations representing Types III and V. These equations are, respectively:

$$\text{Type III} : (1+r_y)^t Y_0 = \left\{ 1+ (1-\alpha)r_y \right\}^t C_0 +$$
$$\left\{ 1+ (1+\alpha C_0/I_0)\ r_y \right\}^t I_0 \qquad (26)$$

$$\text{Type V} : (1+r_y)^t Y_0 = \left\{ 1+ (1+\alpha I_0/C_0)\ r_y \right\}^t C_0 +$$
$$\left\{ 1- (1-\alpha)r_y \right\}^t I_0 \qquad (27)$$

As a preliminary to the investigation of the behaviour of these equations we may, at this point, anticipate the changes which may take place in the behaviour of the principal coefficients as r_y, r_c, and r_i rise and fall under the two main patterns of growth.

To start, we may summarize in a schedule the long-term changes in the coefficients under the two patterns of growth which have been revealed in our

TABLE III
LONG-TERM GROWTH TRENDS OF GROWTH COEFFICIENTS UNDER THE TWO MAIN PATTERNS OF GROWTH

Coefficients of Growth	Type III	Type V
Propensity to Consume: (a) Marginal ($\Delta C/\Delta Y$)	↓	↑
(b) Average (C/Y)	↓	↑
Propensity to Save: (a) Marginal ($\Delta S/\Delta Y$)	↑	↓
(b) Average (S/Y)	↑	↓
Multiplier ($\Delta Y/\Delta I$)	↓	↑
Accelerator ($\Delta I/\Delta C$)	↑	↓
Savings (Investment) Ratio ($S/Y = I/Y$)	↑	↓
Overall Incremental Capital–Output Ratio ($I/\Delta Y$)	↑	↓
Multiplier–cum–Accelerator ($\Delta Y/\Delta C$)	↑	↓

TABLE IV
PATTERN OF SHORT-TERM CHANGES IN GROWTH COEFFICIENTS AS r_y, r_c AND r_i RISE OR FALL

Coefficients of Growth	Type III: $r_i > r_y > r_c$		Type V: $r_c > r_y > r_i$	
	$r_i\uparrow$; $r_c, r_y\downarrow$	$r_i\downarrow$; $r_c, r_y\uparrow$	$r_i\uparrow$; $r_c, r_y\downarrow$	$r_i\downarrow$; $r_c, r_y\uparrow$
Marginal Propensity to Consume ($\Delta C/\Delta Y$)	↓	↑	↓	↑
*Average Propensity to Consume (C/Y)	↓	↑	↑	↑
Marg. Propensity to Save ($\Delta S/\Delta Y$)	↑	↓	↑	↓
*Average Prop. to Save ($S/Y = I/Y$)	↑	↓	↓	↓
Multiplier ($\Delta Y/\Delta I$)	↓	↑	↓	↑
Accelerator ($\Delta I/\Delta C$)	↑	↓	↑	↓
Overall ICOR ($I/\Delta Y$)	↑	↓	* ↓	↓ *
Multiplier–cum–Accel. ($\Delta Y/\Delta C$)	↑	↓	↑	↓

*Invariant

investigations in Part One. The results are presented in Table III, the arrows showing the direction of change—increase ($\uparrow$) and decrease($\downarrow$).

Against this background information of the long-term growth trends of the growth coefficients, we may now examine the behaviour of these same coefficients as r_y, r_c, and r_i change direction. A little experimenting with figures will show the following pattern of changes to hold (Table IV).

For the sake of easy comparison with Table III, the long-term trend of these coefficients under each type of growth has been inserted in the form of the broken middle arrows under each type. It is thus easily seen that the average propensities to consume and to save are insensitive (or invariant) to changes in the direction of r_y, r_c, and r_i under both types of growth. In addition, the overall incremental capital-output ratio is also invariant to changes in r_y, r_c, and r_i in Type V. In other words, these coefficients always tend in the direction of their long-term trend both in the short run and in the long.

We can thus say that the average propensity to consume is *always* falling in Type III and rising in Type V, the average propensity to save is *always* rising in Type III and falling in Type V, and that in Type V the overall incremental capital-output ratio is *always* falling. As to the rest of the coefficients including the overall incremental capital-output ratio in Type III, these may sometimes rise or fall in the short period depending on the directions of change of r_y, r_c, and r_i. Where Type III growth alternates in any way with Type V, the movements of the propensities to consume and to save and of the overall incremental capital-output ratio will alternate, or become mixed in accordance with the patterns of change which we have established.

Table IV also establishes the basic feature of the movements of growth rates under the two principal types of growth. This is that, as growth proceeds, r_c, and r_y rise and fall together while r_i always moves in the opposite direction to r_c and r_y—that is, falling while r_c and r_y are rising and rising while they are falling. This

is the common, though not necessarily invariable, pattern of the movements of the growth rates for any
period of continuous growth. For while this same pattern
of movement can possibly occur in cases of declining
output, it is not a common feature of such cases. The
significance of this pattern of movements in the growth
rates for Keynesian theory will be discussed later. But
it is necessary to point out at this stage that departures
from the general pattern of the movements of growth
rates are more likely to be associated with, or to
precede or follow, declines in the level of aggregate
output. We may now proceed to investigate the behaviour
of the growth equations under dynamic conditions.

The most significant feature of Equations 26 and 27
is that, uninverted, the growth rates r_y, r_c, and r_i
oscillate perpetually within their respective patterns
while promoting continuous growth in aggregate output,
consumption, and investment. These patterns may be
illustrated by means of simple numerical tables from
which are excluded, for the time being, considerations
of the rate of growth of population, r_p.

Table V is constructed on the pattern of an uninverted Type III economy to show the changes that
occur within this pattern over time. The corresponding
illustration is shown in Diagram III a. It is readily seen
that growth occurs continuously in Y, C, and I, but with
cyclical fluctuations in the marginal propensity to consume and to save, and in the overall incremental
capital-output ratio. Nevertheless, the average level of
the marginal propensity to consume tends to fall over
each successive cycle, and that of the marginal propensity to save to rise, thus confirming, for this pattern
of growth, the Keynesian dictum for these coefficients.
This is consistent with the long-period decline in the
average propensity to consume and a long-period increase in the average propensity to save. Furthermore,
the average value of the overall incremental capital-
output ratio tends to rise with each successive cycle
over time, as would be expected for this type of economy.
And, on the whole, the rate of growth of income fluctuates
cyclically but tends to rise on the average over each
successive cycle. These results are in general conformity with the expectations of Table IV.

Table VI is constructed on the pattern of an un-inverted Type V economy, with corresponding illustration in Diagram III b. Here also, growth occurs continuously over time in Y, C, and I (as in an uninverted Type III economy) with cyclical fluctuations in the marginal propensity to consume and to save, and in the overall incremental capital-output ratio. At the same time, the average level of the marginal propensity to consume tends to rise over each successive cycle, and that of the marginal propensity to save to fall, contrary to Keynesian expectations. This is consistent with the tendency to a long-period rise in the average propensity to consume and a long-period decline in the average propensity to save. The rate of growth of income fluctuates cyclically with a tendency to rise on the average over each successive cycle.

In these models of uninverted Type III and Type V growth it is interesting to observe that consumption, normally constituting the greater part of aggregate output, tends to influence the rise of aggregate output more than investment, regardless of the rate of growth of the latter. Thus in Type V, consumption both is the greater part of total output and grows at a faster rate than investment. The overall effect is for the growth of consumption to dominate the growth of income. In Type III, consumption is still the greater part of total output, but grows at a slower rate than investment. Nevertheless, the growth of consumption is, in this case, also the dominant element in the growth of total output.

This result is a significant one from the point of view of the Keynesian emphasis on the dominant role of investment in the growth of total output. Our investigation shows that, on the contrary, consumption, because of its greater weight in total output, rather than investment, plays this dominant role (important though investment may be) and underlines the need for at least an equal, if not a greater, emphasis on consumption in planning for income growth. Tax policies designed to promote consumption (according to the pattern of growth involved) are just as important, if not more so, as manipulations of the rate of interest in order to promote investment.

TABLE V
TYPE III GROWTH: UNINVERTED

Period	Y	ΔY/Y %	C	ΔC/C %	I	ΔI/I %	ΔC/ΔY	C/Y	ΔS/ΔY	S/Y	k	ΔY/ΔI	ΔY/ΔC	ΔI/ΔC
0	40	-	30	-	10	-	-	0.75	-	0.25	25	-	-	-
1	40.4	1	30	0	10.4	4	0	0.743	1	0.257	17	1	∞	∞
2	41.012	1.51	30.3	1	10.712	3	0.49	0.739	0.51	0.261	13.1	1.96	2.04	1.04
3	41.832	2	30.906	2	10.926	2	0.74	0.739	0.26	0.261	17.2	3.83	1.35	0.35
4	42.469	1.52	31.215	1	11.254	3	0.49	0.735	0.51	0.265	25	1.94	2.06	1.06
5	42.919	1.1	31.215	0	11.704	4	0	0.727	1	0.273	17.6	1	∞	∞
6	43.583	1.55	31.527	1	12.055	3	0.47	0.723	0.53	0.277	13.8	1.89	2.13	1.13
7	44.454	2	32.158	2	12.296	2	0.72	0.723	0.28	0.277	17.8	3.61	1.38	0.38
8	45.145	1.55	32.479	1	12.665	3	0.46	0.719	0.54	0.281	25	1.87	2.15	1.15
9	45.651	1.12	32.479	0	13.172	4	0	0.711	1	0.289		1	∞	∞

TABLE VI
TYPE V GROWTH: UNINVERTED

Period	Y	ΔY/Y %	C	ΔC/C %	I	ΔI/I %	ΔC/ΔY	C/Y	ΔS/ΔY	S/Y	k	ΔY/ΔI	ΔY/ΔC	ΔI/ΔC
0	41.012	-	30.3	-	10.712	-	-	0.739	-	0.261	13.1	-	-	-
1	41.832	2	30.906	2	10.926	2	0.739	0.739	0.261	0.261	10.5	3.83	1.35	0.35
2	42.868	2.48	31.833	3	11.036	1	0.943	0.743	0.057	0.257	8.7	9.42	1.12	0.12
3	44.143	2.97	33.107	4	11.036	0	0.999	0.750	0.001	0.250	10	∞	1	0
4	45.246	2.5	34.100	3	11.146	1	0.90	0.754	0.10	0.246	12.3	10.03	1.11	0.11
5	46.150	2	34.782	2	11.369	2	0.754	0.754	0.246	0.246	9.8	4.05	1.33	0.33
6	47.308	2.51	35.825	3	11.482	1	0.901	0.757	0.099	0.243	8.0	10.25	1.11	0.11
7	48.741	3.01	37.258	4	11.482	0	1	0.764	0	0.236	9.3	∞	1	0
8	49.973	2.53	38.376	3	11.597	1	0.907	0.768	0.093	0.232	11.6	10.71	1.10	0.10
9	50.973	2	39.143	2	11.829	2	0.767	0.768	0.233	0.232	-	4.31	1.30	0.30

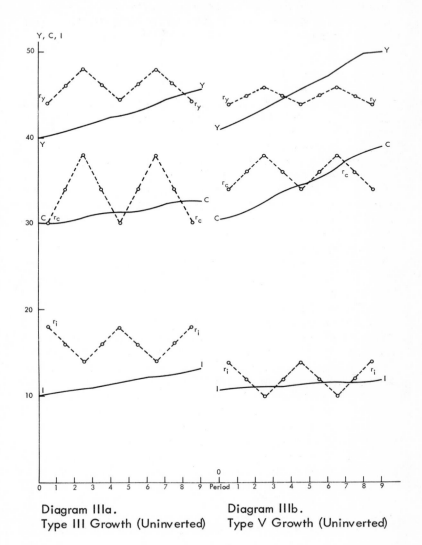

Diagram IIIa.
Type III Growth (Uninverted)

Diagram IIIb.
Type V Growth (Uninverted)

This is especially the case in view of the growing tendency of business to rely on internal financing of investment, rather than on borrowing in the open market.

Inverted Types III and V

The process of inversion is the means whereby an economy is able to change its pattern of growth from Type III to Type V and vice versa. We have already seen the implications of this in Chapter III.

Inversion of an economy can only take place at the steady-growth state, which represents a critical point of transition. For the economy can either pull back away from it, retreating on the opposite pattern, generating thereby the conventional type of business cycle; or cross over to the opposite pattern with continued growth. Simple numerical tables, from which the influence of population growth is excluded, are constructed to illustrate the process of inversion and the resulting changes that occur within an inverted economy.

Table VII with its accompanying Diagram IV is constructed on the principle and pattern of inversion of a Type III economy. All the principal coefficients behave according to the respective patterns prescribed in the schedule given in Table V. The result of the inversion is to produce a Type V economy.

Once inverted, a Type III economy may continue to oscillate within the Type V pattern or re-invert itself once more to its former pattern. We may now examine the results of an inverted Type V economy.

Table VIII shows the results of inversion of a Type V economy with illustration in Diagram V. The long-term trends in the coefficients are in accordance with Table III while the short-term changes are in conformity with Table IV.

All these experiments demonstrate and confirm the patterns of change in the growth coefficients according to the patterns outlined for them in the two principal types of growth, and all are consistent with continuous growth in Y, C, and I without fluctuations, in spite of upward and downward changes in their rates of growth.

TABLE VII

INVERTED TYPE III GROWTH = TYPE V GROWTH

Period		Y	ΔY/Y %	C	ΔC/C %	I	ΔI/I %	ΔC/ΔY	C/Y	ΔS/ΔY	S/Y	k	ΔY/ΔI	ΔY/ΔC	ΔI/ΔC
Type III	0	40	−	30	−	10	−	−	0.75	−	0.25	25	−	−	−
	1	40.4	1.01	30	0	10.4	4	0	0.743	1	0.257	17	1	∞	∞
Inv.→	2	41.012	1.51	30.3	1	10.712	3	0.49	0.739	0.51	0.261	13.1	1.96	2.04	1.04
	3	41.832	2	30.906	2	10.926	2	0.739	0.739	0.261	0.261	10.5	3.83	1.35	0.35
Type V	4	42.868	2.48	31.833	3	11.036	1	0.943	0.743	0.057	0.257	8.7	9.42	1.12	0.12
	5	44.143	2.97	33.107	4	11.036	0	0.999	0.750	0.001	0.250	10	∞	1.00	0
Inv.→	6	45.246	2.5	34.100	3	11.146	1	0.90	0.754	0.10	0.246	12.3	10.03	1.11	0.11
	7	46.150	2	34.782	2	11.369	2	0.754	0.754	0.246	0.246	16.5	4.05	1.33	0.33
Type III	8	46.840	1.51	35.130	1	11.710	3	0.744	0.750	0.256	0.250	25	2.02	1.98	0.98
	9	47.308	1.01	35.130	0	12.178	4	0	0.743	1	0.257	−	1	∞	∞

TABLE VIII

INVERTED TYPE V GROWTH = TYPE III GROWTH

Period		Y	ΔY/Y %	C	ΔC/C %	I	ΔI/I %	ΔC/ΔY	C/Y	ΔS/ΔY	S/Y	k	ΔY/ΔI	ΔY/ΔC	ΔI/ΔC
Type V	0	40	−	30	−	10.2	−	−	0.75	−	0.25	12.5	−	−	−
	1	40.8	2	30.6	2	10.302	2	0.75	0.75	0.25	0.25	10	4	1.33	0.33
	2	41.820	2.5	31.58	3	10.302	1	0.96	0.76	0.04	0.24	8.2	10	1.04	0.10
	3	43.081	3.01	32.779	4	10.405	0	0.95	0.77	0.05	0.23	9.5	∞	1.05	0
	4	44.167	2.52	33.762	3	10.613	1	0.91	0.764	0.09	0.236	11.8	10.5	1.10	0.10
Inv.→	5	45.050	2	34.437	2	10.932	2	0.76	0.764	0.24	0.236	16.0	4.2	1.32	0.31
Type III	6	45.713	1.46	34.782	1	11.150	3	0.52	0.761	0.48	0.239	12.0	2.1	1.92	0.91
Inv.→	7	46.627	2	35.477	2	11.262	2	0.76	0.761	0.24	0.239	9.5	4.2	1.32	0.31
Type V	8	47.803	2.52	36.542	3	11.318	0.5	0.91	0.764	0.09	0.236	7.4	10.5	1.10	0.10
	9	49.321	3.17	38.003	4	11.431	1	0.96	0.771	0.04	0.229	9.0	27.1	1.04	0.04
	10	50.575	2.54	39.143	3	11.660	2	0.91	0.774	0.09	0.226	11.3	11.1	1.10	0.10
	11	51.586	2	39.926	2			0.77	0.774	0.23	0.226		4.4	1.30	0.30

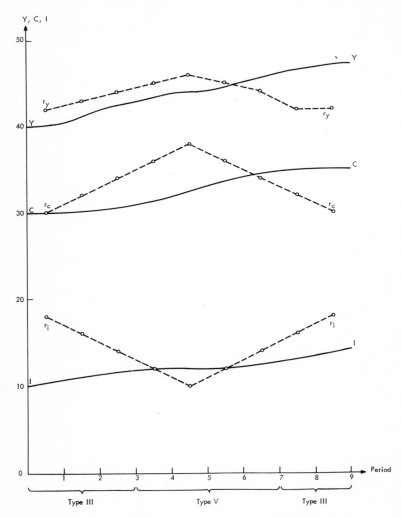

Diagram IV. Inverted Type III re-inverted

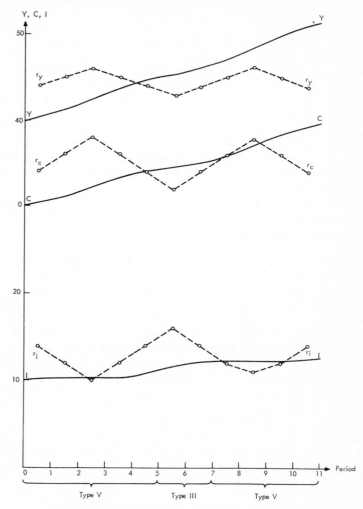

Diagram V. Inverted Type V re-inverted

VII

GROWTH WITH AND WITHOUT FLUCTUATIONS

We now come to one of the most interesting parts of our investigation, as well as one of the most fascinating topics of economic research, namely, growth cycles. A distinction must be made here between, on the one hand, cyclical changes in the growth rates of aggregate output, consumption, and investment which promote continuous growth without fluctuations in the real values of these magnitudes and, on the other hand, cyclical changes in both the growth rates and absolute magnitudes of real aggregate output, consumption, and investment. The former type of growth cycle has constituted the main burden of our investigation and is altogether unfamiliar and unknown in contemporary economic systems. The latter type constitutes the woof and warp of the growth experiences of our modern world.

We have already seen that growth of aggregate income is still possible even with the rate of growth of consumption or of investment being negative. This is the case with Type I and Type VII. But in these cases special conditions are required regarding the external trading and investment relations of the country concerned. However, such cases of growth are not likely to be more than temporary and are, therefore, unlikely to become the basis of permanent and sustained growth.

Having investigated the conditions and patterns under which continuous growth can occur without fluctuations, namely, non-negative values for r_y, r_c, and r_i subject to maximum values of population growth, we may now investigate the conditions and patterns under which a decline in aggregate output can take place, in order to understand the patterns of the business cycle.

Conditions of a Decline in Y in Type III

The usual conditions for Type III growth are the following:

$$\text{(i)} \quad r_i > r_y > r_c$$

$$\text{(ii)} \quad r_i = (1 + \alpha C_0 / I_0) \, r_y$$

$$\text{(iii)} \quad r_c = (1-\alpha)r_y$$

From conditions (ii) and (iii) we obtain:

$$r_y = r_i/(1+\alpha C_0/I_0) = r_c/(1-\alpha)$$

This expression for r_y enables us readily to determine the associated conditions for those cases when r_y is negative and, consequently, when Y declines. These conditions are the following:

(a) $\underline{1 > \alpha > 0}$

$r_y = -\text{ve}$, $r_c = -\text{ve}$, $r_i = -\text{ve}$:
  then $r_i > r_y > r_c$ (Type III/I) or,
    $r_c > r_y > r_i$ (Type V/VII)

(b) $\underline{\alpha > 1}$

$r_y = -\text{ve}$, $r_c = +\text{ve}$, $r_i = -\text{ve}$:
  then $r_c > r_y > r_i$ (Type V/VII)

(c) $\underline{\alpha = 1}$

$r_y = -\text{ve}$, $r_c = 0$, $r_i = -\text{ve}$:
  then $r_c > r_y > r_i$ (Type V/VII)

(d) $\underline{\alpha < 0}$

$r_y = r_c = r_i = -\text{ve}$ (Type IV)

(e) $\underline{\alpha < 0}$

$r_y = -\text{ve}$, $r_c = -\text{ve}$, $r_i = 0$ (if $0 > \alpha = -I_0/C_0$):
  then $r_i > r_y > r_c$ (Type III/I)

$r_y = \text{ve}$, $r_c = -\text{ve}$, $r_i = +\text{ve}$ (if $0 > -I_0/C_0 > \alpha$):
  then $r_i > r_y > r_c$ (Type III/I)

$r_y = -\text{ve}$, $r_c = -\text{ve}$, $r_i = -\text{ve}$ (if $0 > \alpha > -I_0/C_0$):
  then $r_i > r_y > r_c$ (Type III/I) or,
    $r_c > r_y > r_i$ (Type V/VII)

Given, therefore, the conditions under which a decline in Y can set in in Type III, all of them being conditions incompatible with growth, the possible patterns of such a decline are as follows:

(i) A decline from Type III

$$\text{to Type III/I } (r_y = - \text{ ve}; r_c = - \text{ ve};$$
$$r_i = + \text{ ve}, 0 \text{ or } - \text{ ve})$$

(ii) A decline from Type III

$$\text{to Type IV } (r_y = r_c = r_y = - \text{ ve})$$

(iii) A decline from Type III

$$\text{to Type V/VII } (r_y = - \text{ ve}; r_c = + \text{ ve}, 0,$$
$$\text{or } - \text{ ve}; r_i = - \text{ ve})$$

These are all cases of inversion from the first to the fourth quadrant, unlike the inversions which are compatible with continued growth and therefore confined to the first quadrant.

Conditions of a Decline in Y in Type V

The usual conditions for Type V growth are the following:

(i) $r_c > r_y > r_i$

(ii) $r_c = (1+\alpha I_0/C_0) \, r_y$

(iii) $r_i = (1- \alpha)r_y$

From conditions (ii) and (iii) we obtain

$$r_y = r_c/(1+\alpha I_0/C_0) = r_i/(1- \alpha)$$

This expression for r_y enables us to determine the associated conditions for those cases when r_y is negative and, therefore, when Y declines. These are the following:

(a) $\underline{1 > \alpha > 0}$

$r_y = - \text{ ve}, r_c = - \text{ ve}, r_i = - \text{ ve}$:

then $r_i > r_y > r_c$ (Type III/I) or,

$r_c > r_y > r_i$ (Type V/VII)

(b) $\underline{\alpha > 1}$

$r_y = -$ ve, $r_c = -$ ve, $r_i = +$ ve:

then $r_i > r_y > r_c$ (Type III/I)

(c) $\underline{\alpha = 1}$

$r_y = -$ ve, $r_c = -$ ve, $r_i = 0$:

then $r_i > r_y > r_c$ (Type III/I)

(d) $\underline{\alpha = 0}$

$r_y = r_c = r_i = -$ ve: (Type IV)

(e) $\underline{\alpha < 0}$

$r_y = -$ ve, $r_c = 0$, $r_i = -$ ve (if $0 > \alpha = -C_0/I_0$):

then $r_c > r_y > r_i$ (Type V/VII)

$r_y = -$ ve, $r_c = +$ ve, $r_i = -$ ve (if $0 > -C_0/I_0 > \alpha$):

then $r_c > r_y > r_i$ (Type V/VII)

$r_y = -$ ve, $r_c = -$ ve, $r_i = -$ ve (if $0 > \alpha > -C_0/I_0$):

then $r_c > r_y > r_i$ (Type V/VII) or,

$r_i > r_y > r_c$ (Type III/I)

Therefore, given the conditions under which a decline can set in in Type V, all being conditions incompatible with growth, the possible patterns of such a decline are established:

(i) A decline from Type V

to Type III/I ($r_y = -$ ve, $r_c = -$ ve,

$r_i = +$ ve, 0 or $-$ ve)

(ii) A decline from Type V

to Type IV ($r_y = r_c = r_i = -$ ve)

(iii) A decline from Type V

$$\text{to Type V/VII } (r_y = -\text{ve}, \ r_c = +\text{ ve}, \ 0, \text{ or}$$
$$-\text{ve}, \ r_i = -\text{ve})$$

Again, these are all cases of inversion from the first to the fourth quadrant unlike the inversions which are compatible with continuous growth and therefore confined to the first quadrant.

Growth without Fluctuations and with Growing Population

Our treatment of growth cycles cannot be complete without taking into account the growth of population, a factor which has until now been largely, though not entirely, excluded from the picture. This is now necessary because population growth is a variable closely connected with any policy measures which may develop out of our treatment of growth cycles, especially in regard to controlling the conventional business cycle, while protecting the standard and level of living of the population. But first we must see what happens when population is taken into account under conditions of continuous growth.

Table IX is constructed on the basis of successive inversions of Type III and Type V to show continuous growth, with the rate of population growth being assumed constant at 0.02 per annum. The accompanying illustration is shown in Diagram VI.

The table shows that, provided the growth rate of population, r_p, sets the lower limit to the fall in the growth rate of consumption, r_c, in Type III, and to the fall in the growth rate of aggregate investment in Type V, and provided also that control of the growth rate of population is aided by technological progress and fiscal policy in setting the floor to a fall in the growth rate of investment, r_i; absolute growth of total and per capita output, consumption, and investment (i.e. in the standard and level

TABLE IX

CONTINUOUS GROWTH IN Y, C, I AND P

$r_p = $ a constant (say 0.02) $= \Delta L/L$

Period		Y	$\Delta Y/Y$ %	C	$\Delta C/C$ %	I	$\Delta I/I$ %	$\Delta C/\Delta Y$	C/Y	$\Delta S/\Delta Y$	S/Y	$\Delta Y/\Delta I$	$I/\Delta Y$	$\Delta L/I$	$\Delta L/\Delta Y$
0		40	-	30	-	10	-	-	.75	-	.25	-	7.143	→	→
1	III	41.4	3.5	30.9	3	10.5	5	.643	.746	.357	.254	3.937	6.757	→	→
2		42.954	3.75	31.982	3.5	10.972	4.5	.696	.745	.304	.255	3.922	6.386	→	→
3		44.672	4	33.261	4	11.411	4	.744	.745	.256	.255	3.922	5.688	→	→
4		46.678	4.48	34.924	5	11.754	3	.829	.748	.171	.252	3.968	5.045	→	→
5	V	49.008	5.01	37.019	6	11.989	2	.899	.755	.101	.245	4.082	5.422	constant	→
Technological Stimulus (+ Monetary and Fiscal Policy)															
6		51.219	4.51	38.870	5	12.348	3	.837	.759	.163	.241	4.149	6.029	→	→
7		53.267	4	40.425	4	12.842	4	.759	.759	.241	.241	4.149	6.923	→	→
8		55.122	3.48	41.638	3	13.485	5	.654	.755	.346	.245	4.082	8.213	→	→
9	III	56.764	2.98	42.470	2	14.294	6	.507	.748	.493	.252	3.968	7.187	→	→
Demographic Control (+ Monetary and Fiscal Policy)															
10		58.753	3.5	43.745	3	15.008	5	.641	.745	.359	.255	3.922	6.386	→	→
11		61.103	4	45.494	4	15.609	4	.744	.745	.256	.255	3.922	5.693	→	→
12	V	63.845	4.49	47.768	5	16.077	3	.829	.748	.171	.252	3.968	5.043	→	→
13		67.033	4.99	50.634	6	16.398	2	.899	.755	.101	.245	4.082	-	constant	→

Technological Stimulus (+ Monetary and Fiscal Policy)

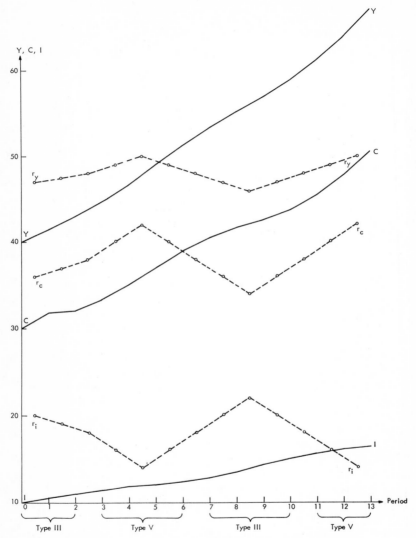

Diagram VI. Continuous Growth without Fluctuations

of living) can go on continuously. Thus population growth and technological progress are the two major exogenous factors in this model as, indeed, in the general process of economic growth. But they are not entirely beyond policy controls.

Demographic control aided by monetary and fiscal policy is necessary for the purpose of safeguarding the level of living while the growth rate of consumption is falling, in order that a floor may be set to its fall. Such should be the policy in the declining phase of the growth rates of aggregate output and consumption (that is, the rising phase of the growth rate of investment). In the rising phase of the growth rates of consumption and aggregate output (the falling phase of the growth rate of investment) the appropriate policy would be to stimulate technological progress and investment and limit population growth in order to set a floor to the fall in the growth rate of investment. When put into effect, these policies would determine the levels of the upper and lower turning points in the growth rate cycles of consumption and investment and in this way the amplitude of these rates can be controlled and the occurrence of negative rates for consumption and investment precluded.

It is necessary to remind ourselves that our basic assumption as well as the basic objective of this model of growth is a continuous absolute growth of real output, consumption, and investment, in total and on the average, and that the policies prescribed for controlling the rates of growth (rather, the level of decline in the growth rates) of consumption and investment are still necessary even if, and in order to ensure that, real output, consumption, and investment, in total and per capita, keep rising all the time. It is interesting, however, to note that the objective of a rising per capita level of real income, consumption, and investment means, in effect, that whether growth is of Type III or Type V, the rates of growth of consumption and investment cannot individually be allowed to fall below, if as low as, the rate of growth of population. In these circumstances, investment and output per worker generally keep on rising. Price level considerations, also, may require fiscal or monetary restraint in combination with technological stimulus or demographic control.

Controlling the Business Cycle

The policy conclusions which we have just arrived at are of great importance for the control of the conventional business cycle. The standard prescriptions followed since Keynes have emphasized the use of two principal weapons—monetary and fiscal policy—both for controlling and regulating the levels of consumption and investment (and, therefore, of aggregate output and employment) and for regulating the level of prices. We have now seen that these standard prescriptions are not enough. Demographic and technological policy must constitute the third and fourth principal weapons for effective control of the level of output, consumption, investment, employment, and prices to be possible.

Table X illustrates the combined application of these four weapons to controlling a business cycle patterned on a decline from a rising Type III to a falling Type V, with Diagram VII providing graphic illustration. These same weapons could also be applied at appropriate points to the non-business cycle model of Table IX, as already shown.

If r_p rises up to equality with, or in excess of, r_c, $\Delta C/\Delta P$ declines to unity and then to less than unity. But this same consequence would result if, instead, r_c declines to equality with r_p or drops below it. Then per capita consumption would decline even before r_c becomes equal to r_p, for in Type V per capita consumption ought to be reckoned net of marginal technological investment. It follows therefore that in Type III growth begins to be threatened the moment r_p begins to approach r_c, unless r_i is pushed up to such an extent as to increase r_y and Y to the point where r_c can again climb ahead of r_p. Similarly, in Type V, growth begins to be threatened the moment r_p begins to approach r_i, endangering investment per worker unless r_c (including in this the allowance for technological investment) can be considerably increased to allow r_y, Y, and eventually r_i to advance to the point where r_i again overtakes r_p.

Considerations of business and consumer psychology have been omitted from our models and discussion, not because these are unimportant, but because our interest in

TABLE X

MODEL OF A CONVENTIONAL BUSINESS CYCLE (TYPE III
TYPE V) AND ITS REGULATION ($r_p = .02$)

Period	Y	$\Delta Y/Y$ %	C	$\Delta C/C$ %	I	$\Delta I/I$ %	
0	40	–	30	–	10	–	
1	41.4	3.5	30.9	3	10.5	5	
2	43.059	4.01	31.982	3.5	11.078	5.5	
3	45.003	4.51	33.261	4	11.742	6	
4	47.253	5	34.924	5	12.329	5	
5	49.318	4.37	36.495	4.5	12.882	4	
6	51.162	3.74	37.955	4	13.207	3	
7	52.565	2.74	39.094	3	13.471	2	$r_c > r_y > r_i = r_p$

Demographic Control, Technological, Monetary, and Fiscal Stimulus

Period	Y	$\Delta Y/Y$ %	C	$\Delta C/C$ %	I	$\Delta I/I$ %	
8	54.533	3.74	40.658	4	13.875	3	Change in: per capita Y = – ve; per capita C = – ve; per capita I = – ve
	(53.482)	1.71	39.876	2	13.606	1)	
9	56.918	4.37	42.487	4.5	14.430	4	Change in: per capita Y = – ve; per capita C = – ve; per capita I = – ve
	(53.880)	0.74	40.274	1	13.606	0)	
10	59.774	5	44.612	5	15.163	5	Absolute declines in Y, I, Y/P, C/P, I/P.
	(53.744)	–0.25	40.274	0	13.470	–1)	
11	63.138	5.63	47.065	5.5	16.073	6	Absolute declines in Y, C, I, Y/P, C/P, I/P.
	(53.072)	–1.25	39.872	–1	13.200	–2)	
12	67.087	6.25	49.889	6	17.198	7	Further absolute declines in Y, C, I, Y/P, C/P, I/P.
	(51.879)	–2.24	39.075	–2	12.804	–3)	

Figures in parentheses show the course of the business cycle unchecked. In this case,
r_p must eventually diminish after a lapse of time.

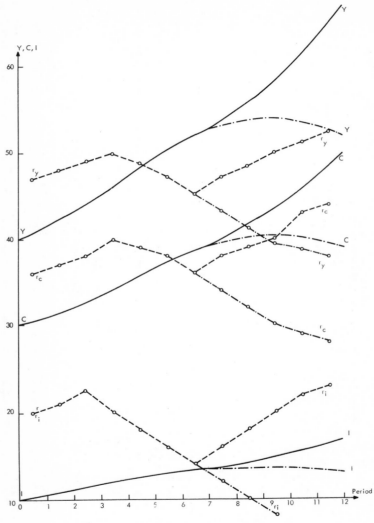

Diagram VII. Business Cycle Control

this investigation, as stated at the outset, is not in the construction of business cycle models. Those models which have already been constructed have amply treated these aspects. Rather, our interest has been in the mechanics of growth, and the business cycle has entered into the discussion only in so far as the mechanics of its generation are involved. With this statement we may turn to consider the implications of our theory for development planning and the setting of growth targets.

PART THREE

APPLICATIONS OF THE THEORY

VIII
ANALYSIS OF PAST PATTERNS OF GROWTH

The techniques of pattern analysis may be applied to an examination of the growth patterns of countries both developed and developing. Because of the technological gap in the latter category of countries, pattern analysis may be applied to its full extent only in regard to developed countries since these possess a tradition of scientific and technological research and development. In regard to developing countries, pattern analysis provides a useful tool for analysing shortcomings in this respect (although the same is true for developed countries). Thus in the present chapter attention is paid to the use of pattern analysis for systematic examination of the past growth patterns of developed countries, the next chapter being reserved for its application to developing countries. In the absence of data on actual volume of technological investment, the figures resulting from the application of our technique to developed countries indicate the order of technological investment appropriate to the rates of growth of the particular countries treated.

The rest of our discussion is best presented in the form of the seven following Tables:

---

1. The data for these tables are derived from the United Nations *Yearbook of National Accounts Statistics, 1963.*

TABLE XI

INDUSTRIAL COUNTRIES' AVERAGE ANNUAL RATES OF GROWTH
OF Y, C, I AND P

	Period	r_y	r_c^1	r_i^1	r_p (max.)	r_p (actual)	r_w (min.)	r_w (actual)	Type of Growth
E.E.C. Countries									
Belgium	1951–59	0.026	0.022	0.048	0.021	0.006	0.005	0.020	Type III
	1954–61	0.029	0.027	0.041	0.024	0.006	0.005	0.023	
France	1951–59	0.042	0.039	0.056	0.033	0.010	0.009	0.032	Type III
	1953–61	0.047	0.040	0.084	0.038	0.010	0.009	0.037	
Germany (West)	1951–59	0.073	0.068	0.086	0.045	0.012	0.028	0.061	Type III
	1953–61	0.070	0.067	0.078	0.044	0.013	0.026	0.057	
Italy	1951–59	0.057	0.046	0.103	0.043	0.005	0.014	0.052	Type III
	1953–61	0.060	0.047	0.126	0.048	0.006	0.012	0.054	
Luxembourg	1953–58	0.033	0.040	*0.015	0.020)# 0.017)	0.006	0.013)# 0.016)	0.027	Type V
Netherlands	1951–59	0.046	0.038	0.073	0.032	0.012	0.014	0.034	Type III
	1953–61	0.048	0.042	0.066	0.032	0.014	0.016	0.034	
Other									
Canada	1951–59	0.037	0.044	§ 0.017	0.024)# 0.019)	0.028	0.013)# 0.018)	0.009	Type V
	1953–61	0.036	0.037	0.031	0.029)# 0.018)	0.026	0.007)# 0.018)	0.010	

Denmark	1953–61	0.041	0.038	0.052	0.030	0.007	0.011	0.034	Type III
Japan	1954–59	0.083	0.064	0.136	0.054	0.011	0.029	0.072	Type III
	1954–61	† 0.009	† 0.070	† 0.182	0.063	0.011	0.036	† 0.088	
Norway	1951–59	0.033	0.030	0.042	0.022	0.010	0.011	0.023	Type III
	1953–61	0.036	0.034	0.041	0.021	0.009	0.015	0.027	
Sweden	1951–59	0.034	0.032	0.040	0.023	0.006	0.011	0.028	Type III
	1953–61	0.040	0.035	0.059	0.029	0.006	0.011	0.034	
United Kingdom	1951–59	0.026	0.024	0.040	0.022	0.005	0.004	0.021	Type III
	1953–61	0.027	0.023	0.051	0.023	0.005	0.004	0.022	
United States	1951–59	0.028	0.032	0.008	0.022)# / 0.014)	0.017	0.006)# / 0.014)	0.011	Type V
	1953–61	0.028	0.028	0.026	0.028)# / 0.014)	0.017	–)# / 0.014)	0.011	

Source: Same as for Tables I and II

1 Computed by author

* Should have been in excess of 0.017

§ Should have been in excess of 0.019

† Based on GNP at current prices

The first figure is derived on the assumption that $2 > \mu > 1$, the second on the assumption that $1 > \mu > 0$.

TABLE XII
FRANCE: 1956-1962
(1,000 MILLION FRANCS AT MARKET PRICES OF 1959)

	0 1956	1 1957	2 1958	3 1959	4 1960	5 1961	6 1962
Private Consumption Expenditure	160.1	168.2	170.5	173.6	183.2	193.9	207.2
General Government Consumption Expenditure	34.8	36.3	35.0	37.3	38.3	39.7	40.6
Total Consumption Expenditure (C)	194.9	204.5	205.5	210.9	221.5	233.6	247.8
Gross Domestic Fixed Capital Formation	43.0	47.5	49.8	50.8	54.3	59.7	64.1
Change in Stocks	6.4	4.6	6.0	1.8	7.0	2.8	5.2
Exports *less* Imports	-3.5	-3.6	-1.2	3.9	4.6	4.3	0.6
Gross Investment (I)	45.9	48.5	54.6	56.5	65.9	66.8	69.9
Gross Domestic Product (Y)	240.8	253.3	260.2	267.4	287.5	300.2	317.7

1956-62 (Type III)

$r_y = 0.0472$
$r_c = 0.0408$
$r_i = 0.0726$
$C_0/I_0 = 4.2462$
$I_0/C_0 = 0.2355$
$\alpha = 0.1284$
$\mu = 1 - \alpha C_0/I_0 = 0.4548$
$r_p(\text{max.}) = 0.0361; \; r_w(\text{min.}) = 0.0111$

Consistency Tests (Satisfied)

$\alpha < I_0/C_0$, i.e. < 0.2355

$r_c > r_y(1 - I_0/C_0)$, i.e. > 0.0361

$r_i < 2r_y$, i.e. < 0.0944

Coefficient of Replacement = 1
Ratio of Depreciation to Replacement = 0.4548
Contribution of Technological Investment to $Y = \alpha r_y C_0/r_i I_0 = 0.3545$

Required:

Depreciation $= \mu r_y I_0 (1+r_i)^{t-1}$

0.9	1.0	1.0	1.1	1.2	1.3	1.4

	1.1	1.2	1.3	1.4	1.5	1.6	1.7
Marginal Technological Investment $= (\Delta T)_t = O_t = \alpha\, r_y\, \dfrac{C_0}{I_0}\, I_{t-1}$							
Replacement $= D_t + O_t = r_y I_0\, (1+r_i)^{t-1}$	2.0	2.2	2.3	2.5	2.7	2.9	3.1
Net Investment (incl. ΔT) $= I_0\, (1+r_i)^{t-1}$	42.8	45.9	49.2	52.8	56.6	60.8	65.2
Aggregate Investment (incl. ΔT) $= I_0\, (1+r_i)^t$	45.9	49.2	52.8	56.6	60.8	65.2	69.9
Of which:							
Aggregate Technological Investment $= \dfrac{1+r_i}{r_i}\,(\Delta T)_t = 0.3545\, I_t$	16.3	17.4	18.7	20.1	21.6	23.1	24.8
Aggregate non-Technological Investment $= 0.6455\, I_t$	29.6	31.8	34.1	36.5	39.2	42.1	45.1
Aggregate Consumption (excl. ΔT) $= C_0(1+r_c)^t$	194.9	202.9	211.1	219.8	228.7	238.1	247.8
Aggregate Income $= Y_0\,(1+r_y)^t$	240.8	252.2	264.1	276.6	289.7	303.4	317.7
Aggregate Investment (excl. ΔT) $= I_0\,(1+r_y)\,(1+r_i)^{t-1}$	44.8	48.1	51.5	55.3	59.3	63.7	68.3

TABLE XIII
JAPAN: 1956-1962
(1,000 MILLION YEN AT MARKET PRICES OF 1955)

	0 1956	1 1957	2 1958	3 1959	4 1960	5 1961	6 1962
Private Consumption Expenditure	5,394.8	5,687.5	6,010.0	6,434.6	7,016.4	7,610.5	8,262.0
General Government Consumption Expenditure	868.8	953.7	1,073.6	1,088.6	1,258.4	1,313.6	1,453.5
Total Consumption Expenditure (C)	6,263.6	6,641.2	7,083.6	7,523.2	8,274.8	8,924.1	9,715.5
Gross Domestic Fixed Capital Formation	1,897.0	2,396.6	2,615.6	3,171.2	4,181.0	5,465.9	6,050.5
Change in Stocks	604.9	686.9	- 190.8	751.6	745.8	1,340.5	665.4
Exports *less* Imports	21.8	- 110.1	100.2	- 74.8	- 277.6	- 759.6	- 425.6
Gross Investment (I)	2,523.7	2,973.4	2,525.0	3,847.0	4,649.2	6,046.8	6,290.3
Gross Domestic Product (Y)	8,787.3	9,614.6	9,608.6	11,371.2	12,924.0	14,970.9	16,005.8

1956–62 (Type III)

$$r_y = 0.1051$$
$$r_c = 0.076$$
$$r_i = 0.1644$$
$$C_0/I_0 = 2.4819$$
$$I_0/C_0 = 0.4029$$
$$\alpha = 0.2416$$
$$\mu = 1 - \alpha C_0/I_0 = 0.4004$$
$$r_p(\text{max.}) = 0.0631; \quad r_w(\text{min.}) = 0.0423$$

Consistency Tests (Satisfied)

$$\alpha < I_0/C_0, \text{ i.e. } < 0.4029$$
$$r_c > r_y (1 - I_0/C_0), \text{ i.e. } > 0.0631$$
$$r_i < 2r_y, \text{ i.e. } < 0.2112$$

Coefficient of Replacement = 1
Ratio of Depreciation to Replacement = 0.4004
Contribution of Technological Investment to Y = $\alpha r_y C_0/r_i I_0 = 0.3833$

Required:

Depreciation = $\mu r_y I_0 (1+r_i)^{t-1}$	91.2	106.2	123.6	144.0	167.6	195.2	227.3
Marginal Technological Investment $= (\Delta T)_t = O_t = \alpha r_y \dfrac{C_0}{I_0} I_{t-1}$	136.5	159.0	185.1	215.6	251.0	292.3	340.3
Replacement = $D_t + O_t = r_y I_0 (1+r_i)^{t-1}$	227.8	265.2	308.8	359.6	418.7	487.6	567.8
Net Investment (incl. ΔT) = $I_0(1+r_i)^{t-1}$	2,167.2	2,523.7	2,938.6	3,421.8	3,984.3	4,639.4	5,402.2
Aggregate Investment (incl. ΔT) = $I_0(1+r_i)^t$	2,523.7	2,938.6	3,421.8	3,984.3	4,639.4	5,402.2	6,290.3
Of which:							
Aggregate Technological Investment $= \dfrac{1+r_i}{r_i}(\Delta T)_t = 0.6167\, I_t$	967.3	1,126.4	1,311.6	1,527.2	1,778.3	2,070.7	2,411.1
Aggregate non-Technological Investment $= 0.6167\, I_t$	1,556.4	1,812.2	2,110.2	2,457.1	2,861.1	3,331.5	3,879.2
Aggregate Consumption (excl. ΔT) = $C_0 (1+r_c)^t$	6,263.6	6,739.0	7,250.5	7,800.9	8,393.0	9,030.0	9,715.5
Aggregate Income = $Y_0 (1+r_y)^t$	8,787.3	9,677.6	10,672.3	11,785.2	13,032.4	14,432.2	16,005.8
Aggregate Investment (excl. ΔT) $= I_0(1+r_y)(1+r_i)^{t-1}$	2,387.2	2,779.6	3,236.7	3,768.7	4,388.4	5,109.9	5,950.0

TABLE XIV
UNITED KINGDOM: 1956-1962
(MILLION POUNDS AT MARKET PRICES OF 1958)

	0 1956	1 1957	2 1958	3 1959	4 1960	5 1961	6 1962
Private Consumption Expenditure	14,522	14,811	15,179	15,838	16,441	16,772	17,004
General Government Consumption Expenditure	3,954	3,851	3,795	3,828	3,898	4,098	4,188
Total Consumption Expenditure (C)	18,476	18,662	18,974	19,666	20,339	20,870	21,192
Gross Domestic Fixed Capital Formation	3,246	3,409	3,429	3,708	4,092	4,460	4,360
Change in Stocks	243	242	100	174	592	297	96
Exports *less* Imports	242	236	109	- 66	- 451	- 281	- 334
Gross Investment (I)	3,731	3,887	3,638	3,816	4,233	4,476	4,122
Gross Domestic Product (Y)	22,207	22,549	22,612	23,482	24,572	25,346	25,314

1956-62 (Type V)

$r_y = 0.022$
$r_c = 0.047$
$r_i = 0.016$
$I_0/C_0 = 0.2019$
$\alpha = 1.1459$

Consistency Tests (not Satisfied)

$\alpha \not< 0.5$

$r_c \not< r_y (1+0.5\, I_0/C_0)$, i.e. $\not< 0.024$

$r_i > 0.5\, r_y$, i.e. > 0.011

The data for Consumption Expenditure and the Obsolescence Coefficient for the period 1956-62 are apparently not in a consistent relationship for a Type V growth pattern.

1959-62 (Type III)

$r_y = 0.0253$
$r_c = 0.0252$
$r_i = 0.026$
$C_0/I_0 = 5.1536$
$I_0/C_0 = 0.194$
$\alpha = 0.0051$
$\mu = 1 - \alpha\, C_0/I_0 = 0.9737$
$r_p(\text{max.}) = 0.0204; \quad r_w(\text{min.}) = 0.0049$

Consistency Tests (Satisfied)

$\alpha < I_0/C_0$, i.e. < 0.194

$r_c > r_y (1-I_0/C_0)$, i.e. > 0.0204

$r_i < 2\, r_y$, i.e. < 0.0506

Coefficient of Replacement = 1
Ratio of Depreciation to Replacement = 0.9737
Contribution of Technological Investment to $Y = \alpha\, r_y C_0/r_i I_0 = 0.0256$

Required:

Depreciation $= \mu\, r_y I_0 (1+r_i)^{t-1}$	91.6	94.0	96.5	99.0
Marginal Technological Investment $= (\Delta T)_t = O_t = \alpha\, r_y \dfrac{C_0}{I_0} I_{t-1}$	2.5	2.5	2.6	2.7
Replacement $= D_t + O_t = r_y I_0 (1+r_i)^{t-1}$	94.1	96.5	99.1	101.6
Net Investment (incl. ΔT) $= I_0 (1+r_i)^{t-1}$	3,719.3	3,816.0	3,915.4	4,017.4
Aggregate Investment (incl. ΔT) $= I_0 (1+r_i)^t$	3,816	3,915.4	4,017.4	4,122
Of which:				
Aggregate Technological Investment $= \dfrac{1+r_i}{r_i}(\Delta T)_t = 0.0256\, I_t$	97.7	100.2	102.8	105.5
Aggregate non-Technological Investment $= 0.9744\, I_t$	3,718.3	3,815.2	3,914.6	4,016.5
Aggregate Consumption (excl. ΔT) $= C_0 (1+r_c)^t$	19,666	20,161	20,670	21,192
Aggregate Income $= Y_0 (1+r_y)^t$	23,482	24,077	24,687	25,314
Aggregate Investment (excl. ΔT) $= I_0 (1+r_y)(1+r_i)^{t-1}$	3,813.5	3,912.9	4,014.8	4,119.3

TABLE XV
CANADA: 1956-1962
(MILLION DOLLARS AT MARKET PRICES OF 1957)

	0 1956	1 1957	2 1958	3 1959	4 1960	5 1961	6 1962
Private Consumption Expenditure	19,473	20,069	20,703	21,698	22,351	23,081	23,947
General Government Consumption Expenditure	4,544	4,452	4,598	4,588	4,697	4,892	4,975
Total Consumption Expenditure (C)	24,017	24,521	25,301	26,286	27,048	27,973	28,922
Gross Domestic Fixed Capital Formation	8,137	8,586	8,261	8,048	7,775	7,712	8,016
Change in Stocks	1,053	210	- 284	400	298	- 134	546
Exports *less* Imports	-1,122	- 885	- 382	- 825	- 533	- 34	147
Residual Error	- 146	- 29	- 99	30	92	140	203
Gross Investment (I)	7,922	7,882	7,496	7,653	7,632	7,684	8,912
Gross Domestic Product (Y)	31,939	32,403	32,797	33,939	34,680	35,657	37,834

1956–62 (Type V)

r_y = 0,0286
r_c = 0,0315
r_i = 0,0198
I_0/C_0 = 0,3298
α = 0,3076
μ = 1-2 α = 0.3848
r_p(max.) = r_w(min.) = 0,0143

Consistency Tests (Satisfied)

$\alpha < 0.5$

$r_c < r_y (1+0,5\ I_0/C_0)$, i.e. < 0,0333

$r_i > 0.5\ r_y$, i.e. > 0,0143

Coefficient of Replacement = $\mu + \alpha$ = 0,6924
Ratio of Depreciation to Replacement = 0,5557
Contribution of Technological Investment to Y = α = 0.3076

Required:

	85	87	89	91	92	94	96
Depreciation $(1-2\alpha)r_y I_{t-1}$	68	70	71	72	74	75	77
Marginal Technological Investment $= (\Delta T)_t = O_t = \alpha r_y I_{t-1}$	154	157	160	163	166	170	173
Replacement $= r_i I_{t-1}$	7,768	7,922	8,079	8,239	8,403	8,569	8,739
Net Investment (excl. ΔT) $= I_0(1+r_y)(1+r_i)^{t-1}$	7,990	8,149	8,310	8,475	8,643	8,814	8,989
Aggregate Investment (incl. ΔT) $= I_0(1+r_y)(1+r_i)^{t-1}$							
Of which:							
Aggregate Technological Investment $= \dfrac{1+r_y}{r_y}(\Delta T)_t = 0.3076\,\dot{I}_t$	2,458	2,507	2,556	2,607	2,659	2,711	2,765
Aggregate non-Technological Investment $= 0.6924\,\dot{I}_t$	5,532	5,642	5,754	5,868	5,984	6,103	6,224
Aggregate Consumption (excl. ΔT) $= C_0(1+r_y)(1+r_c)^{t-1}$	23,950	24,704	25,482	26,283	27,110	27,962	28,842
Aggregate Income $= Y_0(1+r_y)^t$	31,939	32,852	33,794	34,762	35,757	36,781	37,834
Aggregate Consumption (incl. ΔT) $= C_0(1+r_c)^t$	24,017	24,773	25,552	26,356	27,185	28,040	28,922
Aggregate Investment (excl. ΔT) $= I_0(1+r_i)^t$	7,922	8,079	8,239	8,403	8,569	8,739	8,912

TABLE XVI
FEDERAL REPUBLIC OF GERMANY: 1956-1962
(1,000 MILLION DEUTSCHE MARK AT MARKET PRICES OF 1954)

	0 1956	1 1957	2 1958	3 1959	4 1960	5 1961	6 1962
Private Consumption Expenditure	113.5	120.4	126.2	133.0	152.4	162.8	172.0
General Government Consumption Expenditure	23.2	24.2	26.2	28.4	32.8	35.7	39.6
Total Consumption Expenditure (C)	136.7	144.6	152.4	161.4	185.2	198.5	211.6
Gross Domestic Fixed Capital Formation	42.4	42.6	45.2	51.0	60.0	65.6	69.2
Change in Stocks	3.9	5.1	3.4	4.1	8.2	5.5	5.0
Exports *less* Imports	6.7	8.1	5.7	4.6	1.6	- 0.4	- 4.9
Gross Investment (I)	53.0	55.8	54.3	59.7	69.8	70.7	69.3
Gross Domestic Product (Y)	189.5	200.3	206.7	221.1	255.0	169.2	280.9

1956–62 (Type V)

$r_y = 0.0678$
$r_c = 0.0755$
$r_i = 0.0457$
$I_0/C_0 = 0.3877$
$\alpha = 0.3171$

$\mu = 1-2\alpha = 0.3659$
$r_p \text{(max.)} = r_w \text{(min.)} = 0.0339$

Consistency Tests (Satisfied)

$\alpha < 0.5$

$r_c < r_y (1+0.5 \, I_0/C_0)$, i.e. < 0.0809

$r_i > 0.5 \, r_y$, i.e. > 0.0339

Coefficient of Replacement $= \mu + \alpha = 0.6829$
Ratio of Depreciation to Replacement $= 0.5354$
Contribution of Technological Investment to $Y = \alpha = 0.3171$

Required:

Depreciation = $(1-2\alpha) r_y I_{t-1}$	1.3	1.3	1.4	1.4	1.5	1.6	1.6
Marginal Technological Investment $= (\Delta T)_t = Q_t = \alpha r_y I_{t-1}$	1.1	1.1	1.2	1.2	1.3	1.4	1.4
Replacement = $r_i I_{t-1}$	2.3	2.4	2.5	2.7	2.8	2.9	3.0
Net Investment (excl. ΔT) = $I_0 (1+r_i)^{t-1}$	50.7	53.0	55.4	58.0	60.6	63.4	66.3
Aggregate Investment (incl. ΔT) $= I_0 (1+r_y) (1+r_i)^t$	54.1	56.6	59.2	61.9	64.7	67.7	70.8
Of which:							
Aggregate Technological Investment $= \frac{1+r_y}{r_y} (\Delta T)_t = 0,3171\, \dot{I}_t$	17.2	17.9	18.8	19.6	20.5	21.5	22.5
Aggregate non-Technological Investment $= 0.6829\, \dot{I}_t$	36.9	38.7	40.4	42.3	44.2	46.2	48.3
Aggregate Consumption (excl. ΔT) $= C_0 (1+r_y) (1+r_c)^{t-1}$	135.6	145.9	156.9	168.9	181.6	195.3	210.2
Aggregate Income = $Y_0 (1+r_y)^t$	189.5	202.3	216.1	230.7	246.4	263.1	280.9
Aggregate Consumption (incl. ΔT) = $C_0 (1+r_c)^t$	136.7	147.0	158.1	170.1	182.9	196.7	211.6
Aggregate Investment (excl. ΔT) = $I_0 (1+r_i)^t$	53.0	55.4	58.0	60.6	63.4	66.3	69.3

TABLE XVII
UNITED STATES OF AMERICA: 1956-1962
(1,000 MILLION DOLLARS AT MARKET PRICES OF 1958)

	0 1956	1 1957	2 1958	3 1959	4 1960	5 1961	6 1962
Private Consumption Expenditure	278.8	286.0	288.3	304.7	313.9	319.6	334.2
General Government Consumption Expenditure	78.8	82.5	84.0	85.8	86.4	91.7	97.9
Total Consumption Expenditure (C)	357.6	368.5	372.3	390.5	400.3	411.3	432.1
Gross Domestic Fixed Capital Formation	78.2	78.1	72.4	78.9	80.5	79.6	85.5
Change in Stocks	4.5	1.2	- 0.5	7.0	3.4	1.6	5.5
Exports *less* Imports	2.7	3.9	-	- 2.0	1.8	2.0	1.4
Gross Investment (I)	85.4	83.3	71.9	83.9	85.7	83.3	92.3
Gross Domestic Product (Y)	443.0	451.8	444.2	474.4	486.0	494.6	524.4

1956-62 (Type V)

$r_y = 0.0285$
$r_c = 0.032$
$r_i = 0.013$
$I_0/C_0 = 0.2388$
$\alpha = 0.5382$

Consistency Test (not Satisfied)

$\alpha \ngtr 0.5$

$r_c \ngtr r_y (1+0.5\, I_0/C_0)$, i.e. $\ngtr 0.0319$

$r_i \ngtr 0.5\, r_y$, i.e. $\ngtr 0.01425$

The data for 1956-62 are apparently not in a consistent relationship for a Type V growth pattern.

1959-62 (Type V)

$r_y = 0.034$
$r_c = 0.0343$
$r_i = 0.0323$
$I_0/C_0 = 0.21485$
$\alpha = 0.0484$
$\mu = 1-2\alpha = 0.9032$
$r_p(\text{max.}) = r_w(\text{min.}) = 0.017$

Consistency Tests (Satisfied)

$\alpha < 0.5$

$r_c < r_y (1+0.5\, I_0/C_0)$, i.e. < 0.0377

$r_i > 0.5\, r_y$, i.e. > 0.017

Coefficient of Replacement $= \mu + \alpha = 0.9516$
Ratio of Depreciation to Replacement $= 0.949$
Contribution of Technological Investment to $Y = \alpha = 0.0484$

Required:

Depreciation $= (1-2\alpha) r_y I_{t-1}$	2.5	2.6	2.7	2.7
Marginal Technological Investment $= (\Delta T)_t = O_t = \alpha r_y I_{t-1}$	0.1	0.1	0.1	0.1
Replacement $= r_i I_{t-1}$	2.6	2.7	2.8	2.9
Net Investment (excl. ΔT) $= I_0(1+r_i)^{t-1}$	81.3	83.9	86.6	89.4
Aggregate Investment (incl. ΔT) $= I_0(1+r_y)(1+r_i)^{t-1}$	84.0	86.7	89.5	92.4
Of which:				
Aggregate Technological Investment $= \dfrac{1+r_y}{r_y}(\Delta T)_t = 0.0484\, i_t$	4.1	4.1	4.3	4.5
Aggregate non-Technological Investment $= 0.9516\, i_t$	79.9	82.6	85.2	87.9
Aggregate Consumption (excl. ΔT) $= C_0(1+r_y)(1+r_c)^{t-1}$	390.4	403.8	417.7	432.0
Aggregate Income $= Y_0(1+r_y)^t$	474.4	490.5	507.2	524.4
Aggregate Consumption (incl. ΔT) $= C_0(1+r_c)^t$	390.5	403.9	417.8	432.1
Aggregate Investment (excl. ΔT) $= I_0(1+r_i)^t$	83.9	86.6	89.4	92.3

TARGET SETTING IN OVERALL DEVELOPMENT PLANNING

Our investigations have brought us to the stage where the implications of target-setting in development planning can now be fruitfully discussed. As a preliminary to the discussion let us summarize what has been achieved in the general theory of growth and its mechanics, which has been outlined.

We have established the main theme of the general equation of growth, namely, that the process of growth involves continuing growth, at different rates, of the key variables in the general equation of growth, that is to say, population, income, consumption, and investment; and that the growth rates of these variables must bear certain relationships to one another in order to produce the different patterns of growth possible in the growth equation and, at the same time, permit a rising standard of living and of per capita real income. This is the task we set out to accomplish. And in the process we discovered that in Type III growth the saving-investment ratio must invariably rise and the average propensity to consume invariably fall over time, while in Type V growth these ratios must invariably move in the opposite direction, and the overall incremental capital-output ratio must invariably fall. Furthermore, that the conditions of steady or constant rate of growth leaves the magnitude of technological investment indeterminate.

The setting of overall growth targets has become the vogue in countries where planning has been adopted. In many, if not all, of these countries it is usually assumed that output and investment must grow at the same relative rate in order to maintain a process of steady growth, as prescribed by the Harrod-Domar formula. According to this prescription, therefore, once the growth rate of aggregate output is set, the same rate of growth of investment, saving, and consumption is automatically implied. Subsequent analysis is then limited to an explanation of the divergence of the actual from the prescribed constant rate of growth. We have seen, however, that the Harrod-Domar steady-growth state is a special, not the general, case and that the case of unequal rates of growth of aggregate output, consumption, and investment is more generally encountered. Furthermore, because of its possible inherent adverse implications for technological progress, the steady-growth state is one to be avoided rather than made the object of policy.

In effect, a given rate of growth of aggregate output is compatible with different rates of growth of consumption and investment as well as with equal rates of growth of these variables; and, with a given rate of growth of aggregate output, different patterns of growth are possible at different times within the same economy, whether technologically advanced or not. Unless, therefore, the special conditions of steady growth are implied, or, alternatively, one of the two main patterns of growth is additionally assumed, it is not enough merely to specify the rate of growth of total output for any country or group of countries.[1] For if different patterns of growth are possible and permissible, then the rates of growth of consumption and investment, as well as the saving-investment ratio, must also be specified and consistent, as these rates will obviously differ for different countries and according to the rates of growth of their population.

Developing countries may be in the Type III or Type V growth pattern. In the one case their rate of growth of investment will be above that of total output and this, in turn, will be above the rate of growth of consumption. In the other case their rate of growth of consumption will exceed their rate of growth of total output and this, in turn, will exceed their rate of growth of investment. Again, in Type III growth, as we have already seen, marginal and average propensity to save will be rising; the investment multiplier will be falling while the accelerator and the overall incremental capital-output ratio will be rising. In

---

1. It is clear, therefore, that the authors of the prescribed target of a five per cent rate of growth of aggregate output for the United Nations Development Decade had only in mind the special case of steady growth. *(See The United Nations Development Decade - Proposals for action.* E/3613, Sales no: 62.II.B.2 United Nations, New York, 1962 - p. 8.)

the case of Type V growth all these ratios will be re-
versed. And in both patterns the coefficients of productiv-
ity per man and of capital-labour intensity will continuously rise with a given rate of population growth.

These various factors imply different development
and planning policies for the two main patterns of growth,
and for the different circumstances and resources of each
country. Thus it is necessary in Type III, but not in Type
V, to plan for a rise in the investment ratio in both the
long period and the short, in order to achieve overall
growth. But it is also necessary to remember that this
rise in the investment coefficient may take a longer or
shorter period of time, depending on the values of the
other parameters of the growth equation, and even then
only on the basis of the necessary technological conditions.
In any case, a dramatic rise from an investment ratio of
4 or 5 per cent to one of 12 per cent or more of national
income, as prescribed by Professor Arthur Lewis, or 10
per cent or more according to Professor Walt Rostow, as
a condition of rapid industrial transition, or the Rostovian
"take-off into sustained growth," is not likely to be
achieved in 10 years or less, which is the normal period
of most development plans. For example, an economy
growing at the rate of 5 per cent per annum of Type III
with a population growth of 2 per cent per annum will take
from 26 years to 232 years to grow from an investment
ratio of 4 per cent (of gross or of net national income) to
one of 12 per cent, according as its depreciation coefficient varies from 10 to 90 per cent of replacement per
annum. In general, the higher the depreciation ratio the
longer the time required to raise the investment ratio
from a given figure. This is because the marginal technological investment required for growth varies inversely
with the depreciation coefficient, so that a lower depreciation coefficient implies a higher marginal technological
investment and a shorter period for raising the investment
coefficient.

The chances are that in many developing countries
the accumulation of capital may be very slow at first
because of the high rate of actual depreciation (whether
repaired or not) owing to a low level of skills and
technical competence in the handling of equipment.

But the rate of accumulation may accelerate later as the actual depreciation ratio falls with a subsequent improvement in technical skills and competence.

Similarly, in order to achieve a 12 per cent investment ratio on a 10 per cent depreciation basis and a 5 per cent growth rate of aggregate output, it would take 50 years starting from an investment ratio of 1.2 per cent, 40 years from an investment ratio of 2.2 per cent, 20 years from a ratio of 5.2 per cent, 15 years from a ratio of 6.4 per cent, and 10 years from a ratio of 7.9 per cent. In general, the time required to achieve a given investment coefficient will be shorter the higher the base investment coefficient from which a given economy starts. Assuming, therefore, that the British and American economies developed entirely or mainly on a Type III pattern during the first industrial revolution, we can thus explain why it took them over a century before they could achieve their present investment ratio of between 12 and 20 per cent. They, presumably, may have started from an investment ratio of around 4 or 5 per cent (or not much different) with a depreciation coefficient closer to 90 than to 10 per cent and a growth rate of aggregate real output averaging in the neighbourhood of 5 per cent.

By contrast, under the Type V growth pattern it will be necessary to plan for a falling investment ratio while aggregate output is growing, as this decline in the ratio is an inevitable feature of this pattern of growth — unlike Type III where the ratio inevitably increases, but at a rate less than that of aggregate output. Thus an economy growing on the Type V pattern at the rate of 5 per cent per annum with a growth rate of population of 2 per cent will have no need to raise its savings (or investment) ratio nor, for that matter, its overall incremental capital-output ratio, from whatever figure it started out with. Rather, this ratio will decline over time. If, for example, the investment ratio was 10 per cent at the outset, the depreciation coefficient 1.4, investment 10, and consumption 90, then in 5 years investment would have grown, at 3 per cent per annum, to 11.59, but the investment coefficient would have declined steadily at 1.9 per cent per annum over the 5-year period to a figure of 9.1 per cent. Thus the need for savings to be invested is not as great under Type V as it is under Type III. In the former case investment must increase but as a steadily declining proportion of aggregate output. In the latter case an increasing amount as well as an increasing proportion of aggregate output must be invested every year, the rate of increase of the investment coefficient being less than that of aggregate output.

Even in Type III growth, however, a high investment ratio is no guarantee of industrial growth nor, for that matter, in Type V where the ratio is bound to decline over time, unless there is at the same time a scientific and technological tradition. Many developing countries of today could conceivably raise their investment ratio to 12 per cent or more within a decade, and many of them have ratios in excess of 12 per cent, but this does not necessarily spell sustained industrial growth. It is the absence of the technological prerequisites which still makes their 12-per-cent-plus investment ratio not very productive in many developing countries, since they still have to depend overwhelmingly on the importation of capital and technical skills.

All the foregoing considerations show that target-setting in development planning is much less of a simple affair than the Harrod-Domar formula would seem to indicate, and that there is ample scope for the selection of alternative but consistent targets on the basis of the general equation of growth, all this depending on the pattern of growth which a country is following or has decided to follow.

Table XVIII has been constructed in order to illustrate the different targets which may be set in overall development planning under the alternative patterns of growth on the basis of an assumed rate of growth of real GDP (or GAP) of 5 per cent at constant prices, and a population growth rate of 2 per cent. A development plan period of 10 years is also assumed.

Certain conclusions may be drawn from the table. First, it is obvious that in both Types III and V a higher depreciation coefficient (that is, a lower technological coefficient) makes for a lower marginal and total technological investment, and *vice versa*. Second, in a Type III economy, a higher depreciation (or lower technological)

TABLE XVIII
ALTERNATIVE PLAN TARGETS

		Type III		Type V	
Period (in years)	0	10		10	
r_p	0.02	0.02	0.02	0.02	0.02
μ	–	0.9	0.1	0.9	0.1
α	–	0.0042	0.0375	0.05	0.45
r_y	0.05	0.05	0.05	0.05	0.05
r_c	–	0.0498	0.0481	0.0501	0.0509
r_i	–	0.055	0.095	0.0475	0.0275
Y	250	407.2	407.2	407.2	407.2
C	240	390.2	383.9	391.3	394.3
I	10	17.08	24.78	15.91	13.12
$\Delta C / \Delta Y$	–	0.954	0.909	0.963	0.985
C/Y	0.96	0.958	0.943	0.961	0.968
$\Delta S / \Delta Y = \Delta I / \Delta Y$	–	0.046	0.111	0.037	0.018
$S/Y = I/Y$	0.04	0.042	0.061	0.039	0.032
$\Delta Y / \Delta I$	–	21.8	9.0	26.9	55.2
$\Delta I / \Delta C$	–	0.0481	0.122	0.0386	0.0184
$\Delta Y / \Delta C$	–	1.05	1.1	1.04	1.02
$I / \Delta Y$	0.8	0.84	1.22	0.78	0.64
Time required for $I/Y = 0.12$		231.6	26.2	–	–
$r_{(Y/P)}$	–	0.0294	0.0294	0.0294	0.0294
$r_{(Y) \, net}$	–	0.03	0.03	0.03	0.03
$r_{(C/P)}$	–	0.0292	0.0275	0.0295	0.0303
$r_{(C) \, net}$	–	0.0298	0.0281	0.0301	0.0309
$r_{(I/P)}$	–	0.0343	0.0735	0.027	0.0074
$r_{(I) \, net}$	–	0.035	0.075	0.0275	0.0075
D_t		0.729	0.113	0.683	0.064
$(\Delta T)_t = O_t$		0.082	1.018	0.038	0.287
R_t		0.81	1.132	0.721	0.351
N_t (excl. ΔT) = N_t		16.11	21.7	15.18	12.765
N_t (incl. ΔT) = $\dot{N}_t$		16.19	22.63	15.22	13.04
$\dot{I}_t$		17.08	24.78	15.94	13.40
T_t		1.573	11.733	0.797	6.031
$\dot{I}_t - T_t$		15.51	13.05	15.14	7.37
$\dot{C}_t$		390.2	383.9	391.3	393.9
Y_t		407.2	407.2	407.2	407.2
$\dot{I}_t$		17.0	23.76	15.91	13.12
K_t		341.6	495.6	326.6	332.9

coefficient will also result in a lower volume of gross investment and *vice versa*. In a Type V, however, a higher depreciation (or lower technological) coefficient will result in a higher volume of gross investment.

Third, it is clear that, given equal rates of growth of aggregate output and equal depreciation coefficients, a Type III economy will always tend to have a proportionally higher investment bill than a Type V, the proportion tending to be greater the lower the depreciation coefficient. Consequently, a Type III economy tends to outstrip a Type V in investment activity the lower the depreciation coefficient in both cases. This is generally due to the fact that the investment ratio tends to rise in a Type III, but fall in a Type V, economy over time. In general, the higher the depreciation coefficient in both types, the slower the rise of the investment coefficient in a Type III, and the slower its fall in a Type V, given equal rates of growth of aggregate output over time.

A fourth important conclusion with regard to developing economies that make little or no provision for technological investment (i.e., Technological Research and Development) is that they tend to over-invest in non-technological capital equipment (or capital equipment for current production) to the neglect of investment in human capital of the kind necessary to promote technological investment. Not that investment in human capital, as such, is neglected. For it is generally the case that a high priority, as well as a high proportion of total investment, is given to education and social services, especially with the stimulus that comes with political independence for a larger measure of educational expenditures to promote literacy and an improvement of the quality of the population. However, the investment in human capital tends usually to be misallocated, even in the field of education, very little going to scientific and technical education, to the equipment of research laboratories for experimentation, and for analysis of the properties of local resources with a view to the increase of total production based on such resources; for example, in connection with import substitution based on the use of local resources.

Development, both economic and social, starts not with the importation of capital equipment in increasingly greater quantities, but in the minds of men and in the improvement of their manual skills. For, otherwise, developing countries must face the dilemma that lack of skill and technological know-how makes it difficult to maintain the latest equipment which may be imported from abroad and tends to result in a high rate of depreciation. When equipment breaks down it cannot be repaired locally. Technicians and parts must continue to be imported. Thus it may be possible to develop, after a fashion, on the basis of imported equipment and technical skills, but this type of development will always be superficial, not home-grown or rooted firmly in the local environment. Countries developing on this basis tend to continue to be passengers on, instead of contributors to, industrial progress.

There is the widespread fallacy of the advantage of late-comers to industrial progress which asserts that these may, by making use of the most modern techniques and equipment, shorten the period of development and even outstrip earlier industrialized countries. Nothing could be more deceptive or further from the truth. For the essential requirement is often glossed over, namely, the existence of a tradition of technological progress and a minimum heritage of scientific tradition. Unless this exists as a prior condition, it is difficult to see how scientifically backward countries could understand the processes, much less make skillful use, of the latest in technology and equipment. To make the point with greater keenness, the difference is between a nation that could rebuild its industrial equipment if all its capital stock were assumed to be suddenly wiped out and one that could not. This is the real test and line of demarcation, between the developed and the underdeveloped—a tradition of scientific and technical knowledge handed down from one generation to another. From this stems all the inequalities—the gaps in living standards and the vicious circles of poverty and underdevelopment of the underdeveloped. It is time the developing countries took more seriously the importance of science and technology and reallocated their "human investment" to greater advantage.

Especially from this point of view, the results of the theory which has been developed in the preceding parts of this book and the illustrations in Table XVIII indicate that, while a scientific and technical tradition remains lacking or weak, the easier path to the industrialization of developing countries might be to concentrate, in the early stages, on the technology for the production of consumer goods because less investment is required to achieve a given level of output (Type V), rather than concentrate on the technology for the production of investment goods, owing to the greater amounts of investment (both technological and non-technological) required to achieve the same level of output, and the longer time (reckoned sometimes in centuries) required to raise the investment coefficient — depending on the circumstances of individual countries (Type III). The advantage of a Type V pattern of growth over a Type III is the economy in savings and investment and the falling capital-output ratio which are involved—a not inconsiderable benefit where savings and investment are in short supply. Thus we see the fundamental soundness of the approach to industrial development through food, textiles, and other consumer goods, to light industries and electrical equipment, to heavy industries.

The time required for a successful Type III growth pattern, however, does not have to be reckoned in centuries if a country is willing, and makes the necessary effort, to increase its technological investment. This requires a rapid learning rate, a sound scientific educational system, and emphasis on scientific and technical research. In this manner an industrial time-horizon rather like that of Germany, Japan, and the Soviet Union could become possible in place of that of Great Britain or the United States.

The analytical tools which have been devised and illustrated in Table XVIII may be applied to working out the overall investment and consumption targets in a development plan by macro-planners. Alternatively, they may be used to illustrate for didactic purposes the shortcomings in existing plans which may have been drawn up without benefit of the analysis of growth pattern theory.   To this end, the development plans of several African countries are analyzed below.

TABLE XIX

ETHIOPIA: SECOND FIVE-YEAR DEVELOPMENT PLAN, 1955/59
(E.C.), 1963/67 (G.C.)

(MILLION $Eth AT 1953 MARKET PRICES)

Plan Targets	Total	0 1955	1 1956	2 1957	3 1958	4 1959
Aggregate Output (GAP) (Y)	12,434.2	2,266.4	2,371.6	2,481.7	2,597	2,717.5
Aggregate Consumption (C)	10,785.5	2,003.4	2,077.4	2,154.2	2,234	2,316.5
Aggregate Investment (I)	*1,634.9	260.5	290.2	323.2	360	401

1963-1967 (G.C.) (Type III)

$r_y = 0.0464$
$r_c = 0.037$
$r_i = 0.1138$
$C_0/I_0 = 7.6906$
$I_0/C_0 = 0.13$
$\alpha = 0.019$

Consistency Tests (Not Satisfied)

$\alpha < I_0/C_0$, i.e. < 0.13

$r_c \not> r_y(1-I_0/C_0)$, i.e. $\not> 0.0403$

$r_i \not< 2r_y$, i.e. $\not< 0.0928$

The Ethiopian Plan breaks down on the ground of consistency in regard to the projected rates of growth of Consumption and Investment. These rates are projected in the Plan on the base year data for 1963 (G.C.), or 1954 (E.C.). The basic data are clearly inconsistent with a Type III growth pattern.

* The total given in the Plan is $Eth. 1696, but in the absence of the annual breakdown of this figure the discrepancy between the two figures is not easily accounted for. (See Pages 77, 79, 99 and 244 of the Plan.)

Source: Imperial Ethiopian Government, *Second Five-Year Plan, 1955/59 (E. C.), 1963/67 (G. C.)* (Addis Ababa, October 1962)

TABLE XX
GHANA: SEVEN-YEAR DEVELOPMENT PLAN, 1963/64 - 1969/70
(G MILLION AT 1960-62 AVERAGE VALUES)

Plan Targets	Total	0 1963/64	1 1964/65	2 1965/66	3 1966/67	4 1967/68	5 1968/69	6 1969/70
Aggregate Output (Y)	4,675	564	591	623	659	698	744	796
Aggregate Consumption (C)	3,658.5	454	472	492	517	542	572	609.5
Aggregate Investment (I)	1,016.5	110	119	131	142	156	172	186.5
Of which:								
Net Investment (N)	876.3	93.1	101.3	112.3	122.2	135.1	149.7	162.6
Depreciation (D)	140.2	16.9	17.7	18.7	19.8	20.9	22.3	23.9

1963/64-1969/70 (Type III)

$$r_y = 0.059$$
$$r_c = 0.053$$
$$r_i = 0.092$$
$$C_0/I_0 = 4.1273$$
$$I_0/C_0 = 0.2423$$
$$\alpha = 0.1289$$
$$\mu = 1 - \alpha\,C_0/I_0 = 0.468$$
$$r_p(max) = 0.0447;\ r_w(min) = 0.0143$$

Consistency Tests (Satisfied)

$$\alpha < I_0/C_0,\ i.e. < 0.2423$$
$$r_c > r_y(1 - I_0/C_0),\ i.e. > 0.0447$$
$$r_i < 2r_y,\ i.e. < 0.118$$

Coefficient of Replacement = 1
Ratio of Depreciation to Replacement = 0.468
Contribution of Technological Investment to $Y = \alpha = r_y C_0/r_i I_0 = 0.3412$

Required:

Depreciation = $\mu r_y I_{t-1}$	2.8	3.0	3.3	3.6	4.0	4.3	4.7
Marginal Technological Investment							
$= \alpha r_y \dfrac{C_0}{I_0} I_{t-1}$	3.2	3.5	3.8	4.1	4.5	4.9	5.4
Replacement = $r_y I_{t-1}$	5.9	6.5	7.1	7.7	8.4	9.2	10.1
Net Investment (incl. ΔT) = I_{t-1}	100.7	110	120.1	131.2	143.2	156.4	170.8
Aggregate Investment (incl. ΔT)							
$= I_0 (1 + r_i)^t$	110	120.1	131.2	143.2	156.4	170.8	186.5
Of which:							
Aggregate Tech. Investment = 0.3412 I_t	37.5	41.0	44.8	48.9	53.4	58.3	63.6
Aggregate non-Tech. Invest. = 0,6588 I_t	72.5	79.1	86.4	94.3	103.0	112.5	122.9
Aggregate Consumption (excl. ΔT)							
$= C_0 (1 + r_c)^t$	454	476.8	500.8	526	552.5	580.3	609.5
Aggregate Income = $Y_0 (1 + r_y)^t$	564	597.3	632.6	670	709.6	751.6	796
Aggregate Investment (excl. ΔT)							
$= (1 + r_y) I_{t-1}$	106.7	116.6	127.2	139.0	151.7	165.6	180.9

Source: Ghana, *Seven-Year Plan, 1963/64 to 1969/70* (Office of the Planning Commission, Accra)

TABLE XXI
MADAGASCAR: FIVE-YEAR PLAN, 1964-68
(1,000 MILLION FMG)

Projections based on Plan Perspective	Total	0 1964	1 1965	2 1966	3 1967	4 1968	1960	1973	% Rate of Growth
Aggregate Output (GAP) (Y)	856.8	155.5	163.0	171.0	179.3	188.0	128.6	238.3	0.0486
*Aggregate Consumption (C)	709.7	130.6	136.1	141.7	147.6	153.7	111.1	188.3	0.0414
Aggregate Investment (I)	143.0	24.2	26.2	28.4	30.8	33.4	17.5	50.0	0.0841
Discrepancy: (1) Y − (C+I)	+4.1	+0.7	+0.7	+0.9	+0.9	+0.9			
(2) Planned *less* Projected I	+11.4								

(Perspective columns: 1960, 1973, % Rate of Growth)

*Including statistical discrepancy.

1964–1968 (Type III)

$r_y = 0.0486$

$r_c = 0.0414$

$r_i = 0.0841$

$C_0/I_0 = 5.3967$

$I_0/C_0 = 0.1853$

$\alpha = 0.1367$

$\mu = 1 - \alpha\, C_0/I_0 = 0.9262$

$r_p(\text{max.}) = 0.0447;\quad r_w(\text{min.}) = 0.0039;\quad r_p(\text{assumed in Plan}) = 0.025$

Consistency Tests (Satisfied)

$\alpha < I_0/C_0$, i.e. < 0.1853

$r_c > r_y (1-I_0/C_0)$, i.e. > 0.0396

$r_i < 2 r_y$, i.e. < 0.0972

Coefficient of Replacement = 1

Ratio of Depreciation to Replacement = 0.9262

Contribution of Technological Investment to Y = $\alpha\, r_y\, C_0/r_i\, I_0 = 0.0426$

Required:

Depreciation = $\mu r_y I_{t-1}$	6.0	1.0	1.1	1.2	1.3	1.4
Marginal Tech. Investment = $\alpha r_y \dfrac{C_0}{I_0} I_{t-1}$	0.5	0.1	0.1	0.1	0.1	0.1
Replacement = $r_y I_{t-1}$	6.5	1.1	1.2	1.3	1.4	1.5
Net Investment (incl. ΔT) = I_{t-1}	131.9	22.3	24.2	26.2	28.4	30.8
Aggregate Investment (incl. ΔT) = $I_0(1+r_i)^t$	143.0	24.2	26.2	28.4	30.8	33.4
Of which:						
Agg. Tech. Invest. = $0.0426 \, I_t$	6.0	1.0	1.1	1.2	1.3	1.4
Agg. non-Tech. Invest. = $0.9574 \, I_t$	137.0	23.2	25.1	27.2	29.5	32.0
Agg. Consumption (excl. ΔT) = $C_0(1+r_c)^t$	709.7	130.6	136.1	141.7	147.6	153.7
Agg. Income = $Y_0 (1+r_y)^t$	856.8	155.5	163.0	171.0	179.3	188.0
Agg. Invest. (excl. ΔT) = $(1+r_y) I_{t-1}$	138.4	23.4	25.4	27.5	29.8	32.3

Source: *Plan Quinquennal, 1964-68* (Commissariat General au Plan, Tananarive)

TABLE XXII
MOROCCO: FIVE-YEAR PLAN, 1960-64
(MILLION FRANCS)

Projections based on Plan Perspective	Total	1960	1961	1962	1963	1964	Perspective 1959	Perspective 1965	% Growth Rate
Aggregate Output (GAP) (Y)	4,497.7	785.8	838.9	895.7	956.3	1,021	736	1,090	0.0676
Aggregate Consumption (C)	3,682.8	680.1	707.2	735.4	764.8	795.3	654	827	0.04
Aggregate Investment (incl. Stocks and Trade Balance) (I)	762.2	99.6	120.9	146.9	178.3	216.6	82	263	0.2144
Discrepancy: (1) Y - (C+I)	+ 52.7	+ 6.1	+10.8	+13.4	+13.2	+ 9.1			
(2) Planned *less* Projected I	-102.1								

1960–1964 (Type III)

r_y = 0.0676
r_c = 0.04
r_i = 0.2144
C_0/I_0 = 6.8283
I_0/C_0 = 0.1464
α = 0.327

Consistency Tests (Not Satisfied)

$\alpha \neq I_0/C_0$, i.e. $\neq 0.1464$

$r_c \ngtr r_y (1-I_0/C_0)$, i.e. $\ngtr 0.0577$

$r_i \nless 2 r_y$, i.e. $\nless 0.1352$

The Moroccan Plan for the period 1960-64 was apparently inherently inconsistent, being based on perspective data which fail the consistency tests for a Type III growth pattern.

Source: Royaume du Maroc, *Plan Quinquennal, 1960-64* (Ministère de l'Economie Nationale, Division de la Coordination Economique et du Plan).

TABLE XXIII
SUDAN: DEVELOPMENT PLAN, 1961/62-1970/71
($ MILLION AT CURRENT MARKET PRICES)

Plan Targets	0 1961/62	1 1962/63	2 1963/64	3 1964/65	4 1965/66	5 1966/67	6 1967/68	7 1968/69	8 1969/70	9 1970/71	Total
GDP (Y)	423.1	431.7	447.4	467.8	489.2	512.2	540.6	570.7	602.7	637.2	5,122.6
Planned Aggregate Investment (I)	48.3	60.7	53.9	53.0	52.5	53.0	56.6	59.5	62.4	65.5	565.4
Planned Aggregate Consumption (C)	374.8	371.0	393.5	414.8	436.7	459.2	484.0	511.2	540.3	571.7	4,557.2

1961/62-1970/71 (Type V)

$r_y = 0.0465$
$r_c = 0.048$
$r_i = 0.0344$
$I_0/C_0 = 0.1289$
$C_0/Y_0 = 0.8858$
$\alpha = 0.2591$

$\mu = 1-2\alpha = 0.4818$

$r_p(\text{max.}) = r_w(\text{min.}) = 0.0232$

Coefficient of Replacement $= \mu + \alpha = 0.7409$
Ratio of Depreciation to Replacement $= 0.6503$
Contribution of Technological Investment to $Y = \alpha = 0.2591$

Consistency Tests (Satisfied)

$\alpha < 0.5$

$r_c < r_y(1+0.5\,I_0/C_0)$, i.e. < 0.0495

$r_i > 0.5\,r_y$, i.e. > 0.0232

Required:

	0	1	2	3	4	5	6	7	8	9	Total
Net Invest. (excl. ΔT) $= I_0(1+r_i)^{t-1}$	46.7	48.3	60.7	53.9	53.0	52.5	53.0	56.6	59.5	62.4	546.6
Marginal Tech. Investment $= \alpha\,r_y\,I_{t-1}$	0.6	0.6	0.7	0.6	0.6	0.6	0.6	0.7	0.7	0.7	6.4

Required:

	0	1	2	3	4	5	6	7	8	9	Total
Depreciation $= (1-2\alpha)r_y I_{t-1}$	1.0	1.1	1.4	1.2	1.2	1.2	1.2	1.3	1.3	1.4	12.3
Replacement $= r_i I_{t-1}$	1.6	1.7	2.1	1.8	1.8	1.8	1.8	2.0	2.0	2.1	18.7
Aggregate Investment (incl. ΔT) $= (1+r_y)I_{t-1}$	48.9	50.6	63.5	56.3	55.4	54.9	55.4	59.3	62.2	65.2	571.7
Of which:											
Aggregate Technological Investment $= 0.2591\, i_t$	12.7	13.1	16.5	14.6	14.4	14.2	14.4	15.4	16.1	16.9	148.3
Aggregate non-Technological Investment $= 0.7409\, i_t$	36.2	37.5	47.0	41.7	41.0	40.7	41.0	43.9	46.1	48.3	423.4
Aggregate Consumption (excl. ΔT) $= (1+r_y)C_{t-1}$	374.2	370.4	392.8	414.2	436.1	458.6	483.4	510.5	539.6	571.0	4,550.8

Source: Sudan Government, *Ten-Year Plan of Economic and Social Development, 1961/62 - 1970/71* (The Economic Planning Secretariat, Ministry of Finance and Economics).

INDEX OF SUBJECTS

INDEX OF AUTHORS